Essenti

The

Northwe

HART, R. et al
The second world war (6) Northwest
Europe 1944–1945

Essential Histories

The Second World War (6)

Northwest Europe 1944–1945

OSPREY
PUBLISHING

Russell Hart and Stephen Hart

First published in Great Britain in 2002 by Osprey Publishing,
Elms Court, Chapel Way, Botley, Oxford OX2 9LP, UK.
Email: info@ospreypublishing.com

ISBN 1 84176 384 5

Editor: Rebecca Cullen
Design: Ken Vail Graphic Design, Cambridge, UK
Cartography by The Map Studio
Index by Alan Thatcher
Picture research by Image Select International
Origination by Grasmere Digital Imaging, Leeds, UK
Printed and bound in China by L. Rex Printing Company Ltd.

02 03 04 05 06   10 9 8 7 6 5 4 3 2 1

For a complete list of titles available from Osprey Publishing
please contact:

Osprey Direct UK, PO Box 140,
Wellingborough, Northants, NN8 2FA, UK.
Email: info@ospreydirect.co.uk

Osprey Direct USA, c/o MBI Publishing,
PO Box 1, 729 Prospect Avenue,
Osceola, WI 54020, USA.
Email: info@ospreydirectusa.com

www.ospreypublishing.com

This book is one of six titles on The Second World War in the
Osprey Essential Histories series

The authors gratefully thank the Trustees of Hawai'i Pacific
University for their generous financial support in the form of a
Trustees Scholarly Endeavors Program grant that has allowed
Dr Russell Hart to work on the completion of this Essential
Histories volume.

Contents

Introduction 7

Chronology 9

Background to war
The road to D-Day 11

Warring sides
A military audit 17

Outbreak
The Allies invade France 23

The fighting
From D-Day to victory 29

Portrait of a soldier
Donald Burgett 61

The world around war
Rationing and retaliation 66

Portrait of a civilian
Brenda McBryde 80

How the war ended
The road to VE Day 83

Conclusion and consequences
'The most devastating and costly war' 87

Bibliography 92

Index 94

Introduction

The Northwest Europe campaign was the decisive military operation conducted by the Western Allies in the European theater during the Second World War. This global conflict, the largest and most devastating war in human history, broke out in September 1939 as a result of Hitler's racist plan for global domination by an ethnically cleansed Third Reich that would endure for a millennium. During 1939–41, Hitler's Nazi war machine overran continental Europe and the Führer's plans for world domination culminated with Operation Barbarossa – his 22 June 1941 genocidal onslaught against the Soviet Union. This total war aimed to destroy both the Soviet Union and Communism, and to enslave the Slavic Soviet peoples for the benefit of the Aryan master race.

On 10 December 1941, Hitler compounded the folly of attacking the Soviet Union by declaring war on the USA in response to the surprise Japanese attack against Pearl Harbor. In the meantime, Great Britain stood alone against Germany, fighting a war of widely fluctuating fortunes in North Africa and the Middle East during 1940–42. During 1943 the tide of war finally turned as the Western Allies took the offensive in the Mediterranean and the Soviets drove back the Germans in the east.

The Northwest Europe campaign witnessed the return to western Europe of American, British, and Commonwealth forces, as well as contingents drawn from the European countries occupied by Nazi Germany. In the D-Day landings on 6 June 1944, the Western Allies fought their way ashore in the face of strong enemy resistance and established a bridgehead in Normandy. Allied forces repulsed all German efforts to overrun the bridgehead, then assumed the offensive and captured the port of Cherbourg, crucial for the long-term viability of the lodgment, by the end of June. Thereafter, in a series of bitter battles, the Allies first captured the key cities of Caen and St Lô.

In late July, after many weeks of grim attritional warfare, the Americans finally broke out of the Normandy bridgehead. Aided by supporting landings on the French Mediterranean coast in mid-August, the Allies swept through France, pushed into Belgium and in early September captured the key port of Antwerp. But during 8–12 September the German defense regained coherence in northern Belgium and in front of Germany's western frontier. It took hard, brutal attritional battles to advance to the German West Wall defenses amid autumn mud and rain. While the Allies achieved several local penetrations of the West Wall, nowhere were they able to punch through the full depth of the German fortifications and achieve operational success.

During mid-December a major German counteroffensive in the Ardennes drove the Americans back in the thinly held Schnee Eifel, but fell far short of its overambitious goal of recapturing Antwerp and thus splitting the Allied front. The Germans followed up this partial success with an even less successful offensive in Alsace; and both offensives simply dissipated Germany's meager reserves of troops, weaponry, and supplies. Hard-fought Allied attacks finally broke through the West Wall during the late winter and drove the Germans back to the Rhine on a broad front.

With the arrival of spring, the Allies launched their final offensives that shattered the German defenses along the River Rhine, and advanced through western Germany into central Germany to meet advancing Soviet forces on the Elbe at Torgau on 25 April 1945.

By this stage German resistance had disintegrated, and Western Allied forces swept through southwestern Germany and into Austria, while also advancing to the Elbe River on a broad front. Hitler committed suicide in Berlin on 30 April and Germany capitulated unconditionally on 8 May 1945, bringing to a close the Second World War in Europe.

Undoubtedly, without the Northwest Europe campaign the Second World War in Europe would have gone on much longer and thus the misery suffered by those languishing under harsh German occupation would have been the greater. Moreover, the postwar 'Iron Curtain' dividing capitalist and Communist blocs would have been moved much further west. For, in the long run, the Soviet Union – which bore the brunt of the fighting in the European theater – would have ground Germany into defeat. The Allied invasion of France, therefore, certainly speeded the demise of Hitler's Reich, which thus endured for only 12 – rather than 1,000 – years. Despite the Anglo-American command disputes that accompanied the campaign, this multinational effort also helped to reinforce the idea of a 'special relationship' between the USA and Great Britain, that, some would say, continues to this day.

Chronology

1944 **6 June** D-Day landings

7 June British capture Bayeux

10 June Germans assume the defensive

14 June Germans begin V1 rocket offensive on London

17 June Americans break-out across Cotentin peninsula

19–30 June Battle for Cherbourg

26–27 June Montgomery launches Operation Epsom

28 June–2 July German counteroffensive by II SS Panzer Corps

1 July Last German resistance ceases in the Cotentin peninsula

7 July Controversial Caen raid by Allied heavy bombers

8 July Anglo-Canadian Charnwood offensive begins

9 July Fall of northern Caen and German retreat behind the River Orne

18 July Anglo-Canadian Goodwood offensive begins

25 July American Cobra offensive

28 July British Bluecoat offensive

31 July Crerar's First Canadian Army becomes operational

6–8 August German Lüttich counteroffensive on Avranches

8 August Canadian Operation Totalize launched

13 August Eisenhower halts Patton's advance toward Falaise

14 August Canadians initiate Operation Tractable

18 August Patton resumes his advance from Alençon toward Falaise

19 August Falaise pocket sealed; II SS Panzer Corps launches relief operation

20–22 August Partial German break-out from the Falaise pocket

21–31 August German strategic withdrawal behind the Seine

1 September Eisenhower assumes position of Land Forces Commander from Montgomery

Early September German V2 rocket offensive begins

1–9 September Allies advance headlong toward the German frontier

4 September Antwerp captured

4–26 September German retreat behind the Scheldt estuary

5–30 September Subjugation of the Channel ports of Le Havre, Boulogne, and Calais

13 September Battle for Aachen begins

17–26 September Allied Operation Market Garden – fails to cross Lower Rhine at Arnhem

2–16 October Canadian advance on South Beveland

21 October Fall of Aachen – Siegfried Line penetrated

6 October Canadian Operation Switchback begins

3 November Breskens pocket cleared

16 October Isolation of Walcheren begins

1–7 November Canadian Operation Infatuate captures Walcheren

26–27 October German Meijel counterattack

8–22 November Patton's Third US Army captures Metz

14 November Second British Army clears

4 December Venlo salient

16 November American advance against Siegfried Line bogs down in the Hürtgen Forest

13–23 November 6th US Army Group captures Strasbourg and advances to Upper Rhine

16–22 December German counteroffensive in the Ardennes makes progress
18–26 December Battle for Bastogne rages
23 December Allied counterattacks in Ardennes begin

1945 **16–26 January** British Blackcock offensive clears west bank of the River Roer
20 January First French Army subdues
9 February Colmar pocket
8 February Anglo-Canadian Veritable offensive clears Reichswald Forest
23 February American Grenade offensive   across the Roer
8–10 March German Army Group H withdraws behind the Rhine
7 March American forces capture Rhine bridge intact at Remagen
8–24 March American forces clear west bank of the Rhine

19 March Hitler enacts a scorched earth policy
22 March Americans cross the Rhine at Oppenheim
23 March Montgomery launches Operation Plunder assault across the Rhine at Wesel
28 March Second British Army breaks out from Wesel bridgehead
1 April German Army Group B encircled in the Ruhr pocket
8 April British establish bridgeheads across the River Weser
17 April Resistance in the Ruhr pocket ceases
19 April Allies capture Nuremberg
20 April German forces in the Netherlands isolated
25 April American and Soviet forces meet at Torgau on the River Elbe
4 May American forces cross Brenner Pass and link up in northern Italy
8 May German capitulation

The road to D-Day

The Second World War became inevitable after Hitler's democratic rise to power in Germany during 1933. It was simply a matter of time before he launched aggression, since his world-view – shaped by racist Social Darwinism, virulent anti-Semitism, and his own Great War trench-combat experiences – embraced warfare as the final arbiter of national evolution. For Hitler, history was the story of racial struggle in which only the fittest race would survive. He believed that an idealized German race of blond-haired, blue-eyed Aryan supermen – Hitler was neither – was destined for global dominance. To the Führer, therefore, what remained was simply when, and on what terms, a renewal of the Great War would emerge.

None of this, of course, was readily apparent to most western politicians in the 1930s. They strove amid the difficult conditions imposed by the Great Depression and the shackling legacies of the 1914–18 War to compromise with Hitler. Circumstances

initially forced Hitler to act cautiously – reoccupying the demilitarized Rhineland in 1936 and effecting *Anschluss* (unification) with Austria in spring 1938. Unfortunately, western leaders erred fundamentally in regarding Hitler as a nineteenth-century statesman whose nationalist aspirations could be accommodated through negotiation. This appeasement policy only encouraged Hitler's aggression, for it reinforced his preconceived notions of his enemies as weak and racially inferior.

British Prime Minister Neville Chamberlain – like many of Europe's leading statesmen – believed that Hitler was a man with whom he could 'do business': in other words, that Hitler would be satisfied with modest concessions. After securing a settlement during the 1938 Munich Crisis, Chamberlain believed that he had secured 'Peace in our time.' Yet Europe's leaders failed woefully to appreciate both the grandiose scale of Hitler's aggressive ambitions – nothing less than world domination – and his eagerness to resort to war to secure these objectives. (Ann Ronan Picture Library)

Hitler's success in acquiring the Sudetenland from Czechoslovakia in 1938 without recourse to war did not, as Chamberlain hoped, satiate the Führer's demands: on the contrary, it fueled the aggressive audacity of his subsequent foreign policy, with Hitler effectively repudiating the Munich Agreement in March 1939 when Germany annexed Bohemia-Moravia. (AKG Berlin)

Hitler was not to be appeased: in fact, he bitterly regretted the Munich Agreement of 1938, where Britain and France postponed a general European war by surrendering to the Reich the Sudetenland region of Czechoslovakia, with its significant German minority. Despite this stunning diplomatic triumph, Hitler rued not being able to unleash his as yet imperfect war machine on his neighbors.

A sea change in the ineffectual western response to German expansionism materialized in March 1939 when Hitler broke his Munich pledge that the Sudetenland would be the last of his territorial ambitions, and suddenly occupied the rest of Czechoslovakia. Denuded of the Sudetenland, which contained a large proportion of Czechoslovakia's frontier defenses, heavy industry, and natural resources, and still numbed by the Anglo-French betrayal at

Munich, the Czechs offered no resistance. This blatant repudiation of the Munich accord angered western sentiment, and it was this shifting public opinion that prodded the reluctant British and French governments to jettison appeasement and shift to a deterrent policy against future German aggression.

Britain and France postured – reintroducing peacetime conscription and doubling Britain's Territorial Army – to give the appearance of meaning business. Clutching at straws, they unwisely made a public pledge to defend the territorial integrity of Poland, the next likely victim of Nazi bullying. Unfortunately, Germany separated Poland geographically from its new allies, which rendered this pledge incredible because there was no possible way for Britain and France to defend Poland. Hitler called the Anglo-French bluff: he did not believe they were prepared to go to war over Poland and, even if they did, he knew that they could do little to thwart his aggression.

The only viable Anglo-French strategic option to stop Hitler was to revive the 1907 Triple Alliance with Russia that had successfully thwarted German aggression during the Great War. Yet Russia was now the Soviet Union and deep-seated suspicion and hostility toward Communism prevented Britain and France from recreating the only alliance that might have stayed German aggression. Instead it was Hitler who concluded the Molotov–Ribbentrop Pact of nonaggression with the Soviet Union, paving the way for German conquest of Poland. In a secret protocol, Stalin agreed to join Germany in dismembering Poland. With this guarantee, Germany invaded Poland on 1 September. Ensnared by their public pledges to defend Poland, first Britain, and then France, reluctantly declared war on Germany on 3 September 1939.

Yet militarily there was little the Western Allies could do but observe Germany and the Soviet Union conquer Poland. This was the so-called 'Phoney War' when British bombers refrained from dropping bombs for fear of injuring civilians – ineffective targeting technology meant that the bombers had little chance of hitting their targets, anyway. The French meanwhile launched a half-hearted offensive into the Saar that crawled forward against minimal opposition and then inexplicably halted. At the same time, both nations frantically mobilized their economies and populations for war, endeavoring to overcome in a few months the deleterious effects of two decades of underfunding, military retrenchment, and cultural pacifism.

Predictably, neither nation was capable of furnishing a balanced military capable of withstanding Nazi aggression when the Germans finally struck in the west during May 1940. Germany had started rearmament several years before its opponents, and the Nazi totalitarian dictatorship had pushed massive rearmament and militarism at a rate unacceptable in the democratic West. Moreover, and this was the crucial advantage, the Germans had gained considerable operational experiences from the military actions they had conducted during 1936–39. In fact, these early German operations had shown deficiencies almost as woeful as those demonstrated by Anglo-French forces in 1940 – but by the latter date the Germans had learned effectively from these failures.

The result was a Nazi military force that, while still far from perfect, was better honed than those of its opponents. The outcome of the 1940 campaign, while not inevitable, was predictable. Aided by an excellent strategic plan, the Germans achieved one of the most stunning triumphs in military history, achieving in six weeks the very goal – defeating France – that had eluded them during the entire 1914–18 War.

Now Britain was left to face Germany alone. The key weakness of the German war machine was, however, its lack of balance. German naval power remained weak in comparison with the Royal Navy and, despite its success in occupying Norway during April 1940, Germany had neither the amphibious assault capability nor the intimate inter-service coordination necessary to invade the United Kingdom. As an absolute prerequisite, the Luftwaffe had to neutralize RAF Fighter Command, but Hitler frittered away German air power during the Battle of Britain in retaliatory air strikes against British cities, rather than striking British airfields and coastal radar stations. Moreover, Hitler, who was (relatively speaking) an Anglophile who viewed his fellow 'Anglo-Saxons' as racial cousins, never wholeheartedly committed himself to Operation Sea Lion, the invasion of Britain.

In late summer 1940, therefore, Hitler turned his attention to what had always been his ultimate goal: the titanic genocidal struggle to eliminate the Soviet Union and Communism, to enslave the Slavic peoples, and to acquire the 'living space' (*Lebensraum*) crucial for the survival of the thousand-year Reich (see *The Second World War (5) The Eastern Front* in this series). Hitler expanded and honed his army into one of the best fighting forces that the world has ever seen and then, in his 22 June 1941 Barbarossa invasion, unleashed it against the Soviet Union. The German armored spearheads advanced to the gates of Leningrad and Moscow, while in the rear areas Axis forces enacted a brutal campaign of subjugation and ethnic cleansing: everywhere, this brutality drove the desperate Soviet peoples into the arms of the Communists.

Prior to launching their amphibious assault on the English coast, the Germans first needed to secure air superiority to protect their invasion barges from the Royal Navy. Luckily for Britain, the determined pilots of Fighter Command fought off the efforts initiated by Göring's Luftwaffe to defeat them. (Ann Ronan Picture Library)

The debacle of Stalingrad was the German army's worst setback of the war up to that point. It was also a personal disaster for those soldiers forced to surrender to the Soviets, since few of them survived Soviet captivity to return home during the mid-1950s. (AKG Berlin)

Unfortunately for the Germans, the Soviet Union could not be conquered in a single 'Blitzkrieg' campaign, as Poland and France had been, due to both its size and the fierce resistance fostered by German viciousness. Overconfidence and ideologically-driven racist arrogance that denigrated Soviet capabilities pervaded the German leadership, and this fueled the error of pursuing absolute and hence unachievable objectives. Thus, the Germans failed to pursue the effective political subversion that had directly contributed to their victory in the east during the Great War when in 1917 they dispatched Lenin to spread Bolshevism in Russia. In 1941 Stalin's unpopular regime remained as vulnerable to internal subversion as had the Tsar's, but ideologically driven German excesses against even anti-Russian Soviet minorities allowed Stalin and the Communists to rally all the various Soviet peoples behind them.

In his arrogance, Hitler had not prepared for the long, total war that was necessary to annihilate the Soviet Union; and nor did he totally mobilize until 1943–44, by which time it was too late. During 1942 the Soviets husbanded their strength as the Germans unwisely pushed deep into the Caucasus and to Stalingrad, greatly lengthening an already overextended front. In mid-November the Red Army struck back, routed the ill-equipped Romanian air forces north and south of Stalingrad, and encircled the Sixth Army in the city. German relief efforts failed as the Soviets attacked across the entire southern flank and drove back the Germans to the Mius River and to Kharkov. Here, German ripostes managed to stabilize the front again.

The war in the east reached its turning point during summer 1943 when Hitler threw away the first fruits of total war mobilization in an unwise and fully

Strategic situation in Europe, 6 June 1944

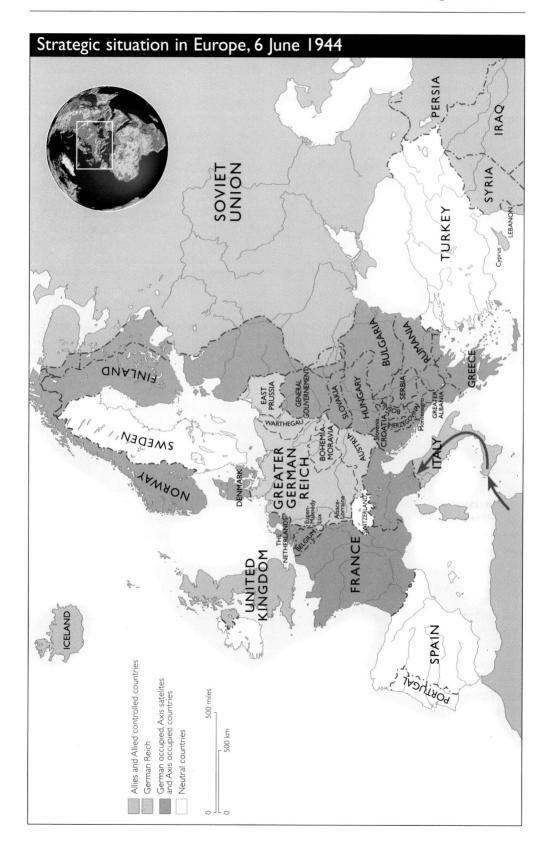

Allies and Allied controlled countries
German Reich
German occupied, Axis satelites
and Axis occupied countries
Neutral countries

500 miles
500 km

ICELAND

UNITED KINGDOM

NORWAY

SWEDEN

DENMARK

THE NETHERLANDS

BELGIUM
Eupen-Malmedy
Lux

FRANCE

Alsace-Lorraine

SWITZERLAND

GREATER GERMAN REICH

EAST PRUSSIA

WARTHEGAU

GENERAL GOUVERNEMENT

BOHEMIA-MORAVIA

AUSTRIA

SLOVAKIA

HUNGARY

SLOVENIA
CROATIA

BOSNIA-HERZEGOVINA

Montenegro

SERBIA

GREATER ALBANIA

BULGARIA

RUMANIA

GREECE

ITALY

FINLAND

SOVIET UNION

TURKEY

PERSIA

IRAQ

SYRIA

LEBANON

Cyprus

SPAIN

PORTUGAL

anticipated counteroffensive at Kursk, which the Red Army stopped dead in its tracks. Thereafter, Soviet forces assumed the offensive all along the front and steadily drove the Germans back toward the prewar frontier. By spring 1944 the Germans were fully on the defensive with attenuated forces and could not now prevail in the east.

Meanwhile, a less brutal war was being waged in the Mediterranean. Hitler had little interest in this theater and was only drawn reluctantly into the region due to the military failures of his Axis partner, fascist Italy. A struggle of widely fluctuating fortunes materialized during 1941–42, but Hitler never committed the resources to overrun the British in North Africa, nor were Axis lines of communication secure enough to achieve this. Hitler's reluctance to commit forces to this southern flank ensured that the Axis failed to conquer Malta, which allowed the Allies to continue contesting the central and eastern Mediterranean.

With their lines of communication increasingly imperiled, the Axis powers were forced on the defensive in North Africa and then, during autumn 1942, were driven back toward the west. Finally, in November Allied forces landed in French Northwest Africa in Operation Torch and began to strangle into defeat the German forces then retiring into Tunisia. In May 1943, cut off from aerial and maritime resupply, the remaining Axis forces in Tunisia capitulated.

The Western Allies, still inexperienced, continued peripheral attacks aimed at wearing down the enemy. Allied amphibious attacks captured Sicily during July 1943 and then secured a beachhead on the Italian mainland during September. The Allies then slowly advanced up the peninsula of Italy until they bogged down at the strong German Winter Line defenses that ran from Naples through the Liri valley. The highly defensible terrain of Italy, the narrowness of the peninsula, and the rough parity in forces committed ensured that the Allies had no real prospect of rapid success in this theater.

The Mediterranean campaign did, however, divert German forces from the west, where since November 1943 the Germans had been desperately preparing to thwart an Allied invasion of France, which they knew would come during mid-1944. For the Western Allies, the decisive campaign of the war was about to begin. If the Germans could repulse the Allied invasion, then they could throw their armies in the west against the Red Army, hopefully halt the Soviet juggernaut, and perhaps still achieve an acceptable negotiated peace. The outcome of the war thus hinged on the Allied invasion of France.

A military audit

The Northwest Europe campaign pitted the armed forces of the Western Allies against the Wehrmacht, the Nazi German military. The combined Allied contingents were called the Allied Expeditionary Forces and comprised troops from the United States, the United Kingdom, Canada, France, Poland, the Netherlands, Belgium, and Czechoslovakia. The American General Dwight Eisenhower commanded the Supreme Headquarters, Allied Expeditionary Forces (SHAEF). General Bernard Montgomery served as the Land Forces Commander during the initial landings until 1 September when the position passed to Eisenhower.

Montgomery led the Anglo-Canadian 21st Army Group, which from July 1944 fielded three armies: the US First Army led by General Omar Bradley; the British Second Army under Miles 'Bimbo' Dempsey; and the Canadian First Army under General Henry Crerar. On 1 August 1944 Bradley took command of the 12th US Army Group with the First Army (General Courtney Hodges)

The heads of state of the three main Allied contingents in northwest Europe: from left to right, Canadian Prime Minister W. L. Mackenzie King, American President Theodore Roosevelt, and British Prime Minister Winston Churchill. (Imperial War Museum H32129)

The Allied senior command team for the Northwest Europe campaign meet for the first time in London in January 1944. From left to right, the team included (top row) General Omar Bradley, Admiral Bertram Ramsay, Air Marshall Trafford Leigh-Mallory, General Walter Bedell-Smith, and (bottom row) Air Marshal Arthur Conningham, Supreme Commander Dwight Eisenhower, and General Bernard Montgomery. (ISI)

and Third Army (General George Patton) under command. When, during September, the forces pushing northeast from the French Mediterranean coast linked up with those advancing east from Normandy, the 6th US Army Group, led by General Jacob Devers, and comprising the American Seventh Army and French First Army, came under Eisenhower's control. Later still, the American Ninth and Fifteenth Armies joined Bradley's army group.

Admiral Sir Bertram Ramsay controlled the vast invasion armada and naval covering forces. Air Chief Marshal Sir Trafford Leigh-Mallory commanded the Allied Expeditionary Air Forces, comprising the Royal Air Force, the US Army Air Force, and the Royal Canadian Air Force. Tactical

aviation belonging to the US IX and XIX Tactical Air Commands and the Anglo-Canadian Second Tactical Air Force supported the ground battle. The heavy bombers of RAF Bomber Command and the Eighth United States Army Air Force provided additional assistance.

The German Commander-in-Chief West, Field Marshal Gerd von Rundstedt, exercised nominal control over the Wehrmacht in France, Belgium, and Holland. His ground

As Commander-in-Chief West, Field Marshal Gerd von Rundstedt exercised nominal authority over all of the German armed forces in western Europe. In reality, however, his three subordinate ground commanders – including Army Group B commander Erwin Rommel – as well as his theater air force and naval commanders all enjoyed considerable freedom of action. (AKG Berlin)

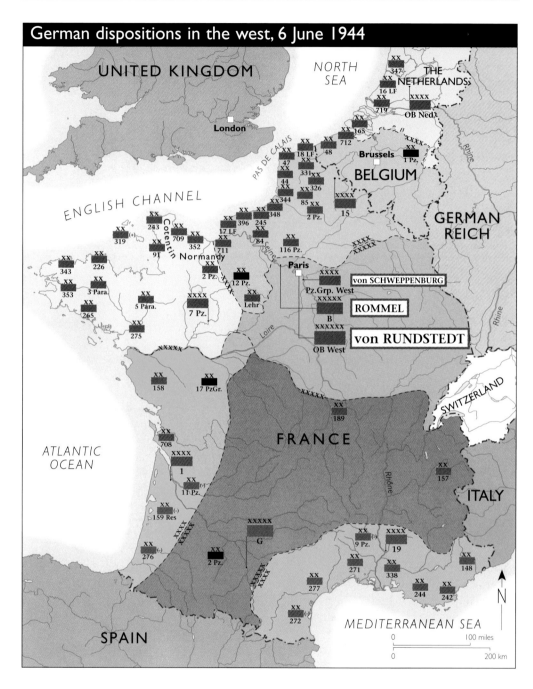

German dispositions in the west, 6 June 1944

forces belonged to three separate commands.
Field Marshal Erwin Rommel's Army Group B
comprised the Seventh Army in Brittany and
Normandy and the Fifteenth Army deployed
from Le Havre along the Pas de Calais to the
Scheldt. The independent LXXXVIII Corps
defended the Netherlands. Finally came
Army Group G, comprising the First Army
deployed along the western Atlantic coast
and the Nineteenth Army defending the
southern French Mediterranean coast.

In addition, General Geyr von
Schweppenburg's Panzer Group West
controlled the mechanized reserves who
were tasked with driving the invaders back
into the sea. Further complicating the

Field Marshal Erwin Rommel – the 'Desert Fox' – commanded Army Group B in northern France and Belgium. He was not impressed with large sections of the Atlantic Wall defenses, and in the months prior to the D-Day landings he channeled his iron determination into strengthening these coastal defenses. (AKG Berlin)

ground organization was the fact that four of the 10 mechanized divisions in the west were designated as Armed Forces High Command (OKW) reserves, and it required Hitler's permission before these could be committed to combat.

Admiral Kranke's Naval High Command West orchestrated the Kriegsmarine's counterinvasion measures. German Navy assets in western Europe comprised numerous small surface vessels, 40 U-boats, and many naval coast artillery batteries. German aircraft in the west belonged to General Sperrle's III Air Fleet. Decimated by sustained aerial combat during 1943–44 while opposing the Allied bomber offensive against the Reich, the Luftwaffe had only a few hundred planes available to defend French airspace.

The Allies had a significant numerical superiority in troops, heavy weapons, logistics, air power, and naval assets. The Kriegsmarine and Luftwaffe might be able to achieve local successes, but they were so heavily outnumbered that they were unable to contest the invasion. Mastery of the skies allowed the Allies to launch an increasingly effective strategic bombing campaign against the German war economy and transportation network. Such attacks had already essentially isolated the Normandy invasion area prior to D-Day, and the dwindling German ability to bring up fresh troops and supplies to the fighting front became an increasingly debilitating weakness as the campaign progressed.

The Germans, on the other hand, would rarely molest the Allied war economy in the last 18 months of the war. Moreover, as a result of the code-breaking successes of 'Ultra,' the Allies had excellent intelligence about German dispositions and intentions, while the Germans possessed a woefully inadequate intelligence picture.

Despite these significant advantages, however, Allied victory was not a foregone conclusion. The Germans enjoyed a qualitative edge, at least in ground forces, early in the campaign – although this edge was blunted during the campaign. The Allied armies in June 1944 had yet to reach peak effectiveness, and so could not yet engage the *Westheer* on equal terms.

Montgomery presided over a flawed British army whose development had been stunted between the wars and had been unable to cope with German offensives. It had therefore suffered serious defeats early in the war in Norway, France, North Africa, Malaysia, and Burma. Only with difficulty had the army recovered from these setbacks and fully learned the lessons of modern war during 1942–44. Consequently, Montgomery was acutely aware that his army's morale remained vulnerable. The army had also only been on the sustained offensive for a little over a year and was still developing proficiency in the complex art of attacking stout German defenses.

Additionally, Montgomery was cognizant of the finite nature of British resources. The nation had already been at war for nearly five years and was conducting simultaneous military operations in multiple theaters across the globe. Montgomery was determined to avoid the catastrophic casualties suffered during the First World War, from which Britain had neither psychologically nor materially fully recovered.

British military operations were therefore dominated by personnel concerns as its manpower dried up. Montgomery clearly understood that all available reserves would be consumed during the campaign and that his command would become a wasting asset. The manpower situation was even more acute for the Canadians, and of course very few replacements were available for the continental contingents fighting alongside the Allies, as they were all forces in exile.

These constraints powerfully shaped Montgomery's conduct of the campaign. He devised a cautious theater strategy where the Allies would use their numerical and material superiority to wear down the enemy in a protracted attritional battle. Montgomery eschewed a bold maneuver warfare strategy that might have won the war more quickly but ran the risk of increasing casualties. The result was a careful and controlled approach to operations that enabled the Germans to organize effective defensive positions as they withdrew.

The American military, on the other hand, had far greater resources. After their setback at the Kasserine Pass in January 1943, the Americans had steadily gained the upper hand over the Germans. Eisenhower's forces therefore had more confidence and better morale. The American military tradition had long emphasized direct offensive action. In fact its aggressive, offensive doctrine ensured that American troops sometimes lacked the respect for the enemy that the British had learned through painful experience. The biggest problem the Americans faced was their inexperience. Only a tiny fraction of the forces earmarked for the Normandy campaign had previously seen action.

Another deficiency was doctrinal. Interwar technological changes – particularly the development of mechanized forces and air power – fundamentally challenged military doctrine in the American army. Despite its endeavors, when it entered the Second World War, the army had not yet worked out how to integrate armor and air power fully in support of ground operations. Combat in the Mediterranean quickly exposed these flaws in doctrine; yet, effective solutions to these problems were still emerging during summer 1944.

The audit of war also illuminated the inefficiency of the American manpower replacement system, which was unable to restore rapidly fighting power to depleted formations. The problem of sustaining combat power was aggravated by the American government's shortsighted decision to limit the wartime army to just 90 divisions, a policy that forced formations to stay in the front line indefinitely, rather than being rotated out for rest and replenishment. A combination of inexperience, doctrinal deficiencies, and a poor manpower replacement system ensured that the US army in June 1944 was not yet able to bring its full fighting power to bear.

Given its greater resources and aggressive, offensive doctrine, the American military naturally assumed the larger role in the campaign, increasingly so as it progressed. It was to spearhead the Allied break-out once a permanent lodgment had been achieved. All the armies of the Western Allies learned through trial and error to fight more proficiently as the northwest Europe campaign progressed, thereby narrowing and ultimately eradicating the German qualitative edge. It was the US army, however, that proved able to adapt and enhance its combat effectiveness most rapidly. By the latter stages of the Northwest Europe campaign, it was able to outfight rather than simply overwhelm an increasingly outnumbered and outgunned enemy. This ability to adapt and enhance its combat effectiveness ensured that the USA emerged preeminent within the coalition by 1945.

Defeating the Nazi military force, however, was never going to be easy or quick. The German defenders had the benefit of considerable combat experience, and a realistic, proven doctrine and tactics refined through years of war. Operating under a totalitarian regime, the military potentially had all the resources of the state at its disposal. Moreover, the Germans were a martial people with a long and proud military history. Nevertheless, the Nazi war machine was by no means invincible; nor were its soldiers the 'supermen' that racist Nazi propaganda extolled them to be.

In reality, the German military fought in northwest Europe under severe constraints. Brutal attrition in the east had already torn the heart out of the Wehrmacht and it was scraping the manpower and resources barrels by 1944. But its biggest deficiencies were logistical. Constant combat ensured that the Germans lacked the supplies necessary for victory and throughout the campaign they operated on a logistical shoestring, particularly liquid fuels. Moreover, the German war economy had long been inefficient and poorly managed. While dramatic increases in production had recently been realized by ruthless rationalization, the German war economy was now subject to punishing Allied heavy bomber attacks and was unable to meet the needs of a three-front war. Consequently, the German military remained perennially short of the means of conducting modern operations. It was rarely able to contest Allied aerial supremacy, which hindered all German ground operations and denied them information about the enemy.

German commanders, therefore, remained woefully ignorant of enemy actions and intentions, which hampered German countermeasures. Attrition had also badly denuded German ground forces of vehicles, reducing the strategic mobility that had hitherto allowed German forces to evade annihilation by a numerically superior enemy. This dwindling mobility progressively increased the vulnerability of German formations to encirclement and annihilation by a far more mobile enemy.

These deficiencies ensured that the German military was unable to mount the combined-arms defense necessary to prevail in the west, and that instead it would slowly be driven back in grim attritional warfare. Nonetheless, the determination of German troops and commanders, their professionalism, as well as their realistic doctrine, tactics, and training allowed them to offer sustained, stubborn resistance that cost the Allies dearly. Influenced by Nazi racism and propaganda, as well as the instinct for self-preservation, German troops continued to fight to protect their families at home from the vengeance that they feared the Allies would exact for the horrible measures the Nazis had taken to keep Europe under control. The Germans could be expected to fight long and hard. And even if they could not win, they could at least postpone the inevitable for as long as possible and increase the price of the enemy's victory.

The Allies invade France

The Allied armed forces required extensive preparation before they could successfully invade Nazi-occupied France. During 1940–41 the British military was fully preoccupied preparing to thwart an anticipated German invasion of Britain. Only when that threat receded, after Hitler's June 1941 invasion of the Soviet Union, could the British armed forces contemplate a return to the continent.

However, other struggles continued to preoccupy British forces. At sea, the Battle of the Atlantic raged, threatening Britain's maritime communications, until the Allies exorcised the U-boat threat during 1943 (see *The Second World War (3) The war at sea* in this series). In the skies, the Allies had to contend with continued periodic German air

Britain had to secure strategic success over the German U-boat menace as well as the German Navy's commerce raiding surface fleet before serious preparations could begin for any future amphibious landing on the coast of Nazi-occupied Europe. (AKG Berlin)

raids across the Channel. Moreover, Britain found itself engaged in ongoing ground combat in both Burma and North Africa – operations that diverted troops and resources away from Britain. It was therefore not until 1943 that invasion preparations hit high gear.

Even then much work needed to be done. The British army commanders had to inculcate the troops with the important lessons of modern war that had been so painfully relearned in North Africa. The army had to reequip with new weaponry; formations had to reorganize to enhance their fighting power; and for the first time, troops undertook offensive training geared toward continental warfare.

British air, ground, and naval forces also had to learn to work smoothly together to establish the effective interservice cooperation that was essential for victory. But building good teamwork required long association to develop full understanding of the respective capabilities and limitations of

each service. Each branch of the army – infantry, artillery, and armor – had not only to improve its doctrine and training, but also to put aside regimental tribalism to work together effectively.

The D-Day amphibious assault also required extensive preparation. Initially, the Allies greatly underestimated the difficulties this entailed. They were rudely disabused of such complacency during the August 1942 Dieppe raid, in which the 2nd Canadian Division was badly mauled attacking a well-defended German-held port. The most important lesson of Dieppe was that a heavily defended harbor was too tough a nut to crack. The Allies therefore decided to land adjacent to a major port and establish a firm lodgment, before seizing the harbor which would be vital to the long-term logistical sustainability of the bridgehead. After considerable debate, the Allies chose Normandy, with its major port of Cherbourg, as the invasion site.

The Dieppe raid also demonstrated the need for specialized amphibious assault armor to crack the enemy's beach defenses; for, at Dieppe, the supporting tanks proved unable to get off the beach to assist the troops as they advanced inland. Over the next year Britain devoted considerable resources to developing these vehicles. Dieppe equally revealed the need for fire support during the actual landing. In the lead-up to D-Day, the Allied navies developed and refined elaborate procedures to deliver naval gunfire during the landings. They built special landing craft, equipped with guns and rockets to augment naval gunfire. Assembling, organizing, and preparing an amphibious armada of thousands of vessels took many months to complete.

The Royal Air Force (RAF) also had an important role to play. Having won the Battle of Britain in 1940, Fighter Command needed a new mission and found it in the direct, tactical support of ground forces on the battlefield. Such support had proven woefully deficient in the early desert battles, to such an extent that British troops derided the RAF as the 'Royal Absent Force.' Initially,

technical problems – including the unsuitability of aircraft, lack of air–ground coordination, and poor aerial recognition skills – seriously hampered the utility of tactical aviation. Only through a difficult process of trial and error were solutions to these problems found. By D-Day, however, Allied air power was ready to provide extensive and sustained tactical air support.

The RAF leadership, however, remained loath to divert Bomber Command from its nocturnal area bombing of Germany's cities, which was intended to break civilian morale. This reflected the powerful sway of interwar strategic bombing theorists, who held that the heavy bomber 'would always get through' to its target and that, consequently, strategic bombing was capable of winning

Air Marshal Harris, head of Bomber Command, spearheaded Britain's strategic bombing offensive against Germany, which was designed to break the morale of Germany's civilian population. During the Northwest Europe campaign, Bomber Command also employed its heavy bombers in direct support of Montgomery's offensives, most notably during Operation Goodwood in July 1944. (AKG Berlin) wars unaided. The result of this dogma was increasingly heavy night attacks by the RAF and daylight precision raids by the US Army Air Force against German industrial centers.

The Germans, however, were unwilling to accept that the bomber would always get through. During 1943 they developed a potent air defense system that involved

Allied aerial interdiction attacks were so successful in the weeks prior to D-Day that virtually every bridge over the Loire and Seine rivers into Normandy had been put out of action. This accomplishment severely dislocated Rommel's ability to get reinforcements to the invasion front line. Of course, when the Allies came to cross the Seine in August 1944, they had to construct new pontoon bridges like the one depicted here in the foreground. (Imperial War Museum B9748)

specialized night fighters vectored onto bomber streams by ground-based early warning radar. The result over winter 1943–44 was the infliction of loss rates that Bomber Command could not sustain indefinitely. American daylight raids also began to suffer correspondingly heavy losses. The solution was long-range fighter protection, but it was not until the development of the P-51 Mustang external fuel tanks that it proved possible for fighters to stay with the bombers all the way to their German targets.

The attrition that Allied heavy bombers suffered over winter 1943–44 had two unanticipated benefits, however. The first was the destruction of the German fighter

force in western Europe by Allied long-range fighter escorts as the enemy planes came up to engage the bombers. Victory in this attritional struggle gave the Allies the aerial supremacy they needed to guarantee success in the invasion. Second, the heavy attrition softened Bomber Command's dogmatic opposition to employing strategic air power in support of the Normandy invasion. Thus, during spring 1944 heavy bombers joined tactical aviation – fighters, fighter-bombers, and medium bombers – in a massive aerial interdiction campaign intended to isolate the Normandy battlefield. By D-Day, despite consciously dissipating their strikes to disguise the location of the invasion, Allied air attacks had destroyed virtually every rail bridge over the rivers Loire and Seine into Normandy, thus severely hampering the German ability to move forces to repel the invasion.

The task that the American military faced was even greater, for in 1943 the US army had very few combat-ready troops in Britain and these lacked the support services necessary for offensive amphibious operations. The USA had only entered the war in December 1941 and sustained peacetime neglect had ensured that its armed services required considerable time to shape up for overseas deployment. Moreover, no sooner had American forces arrived in Britain in 1942 than they were immediately committed to combat in the Mediterranean during Operation Torch, the November 1942 invasion of French northwest Africa. After eventual victory in Tunisia during May 1943, in what proved a difficult baptism of fire for inexperienced American forces, US troops helped capture Sicily during July–August 1943 and then invaded Italy that September.

It was therefore not until the autumn of 1943 that veteran formations could be withdrawn from the Mediterranean to prepare for Operation Overlord, as the Normandy invasion had now been designated. In the meantime, a massive build-up of American forces in Britain occurred, including the enormous quantities of ordnance, ammunition, fuel, rations, and spare parts needed to sustain operations. American forces gathered in western England adjacent to their ports of arrival, and logistic considerations more than anything else determined that American forces would land on the right (western) flank of the invasion.

American troops also worked hard in the year before D-Day to overcome the flaws in their combat performance demonstrated in the Mediterranean. The biggest weakness in that theater had been the inadequate tactical air support caused by the lack of air–ground communication, poor aerial recognition skills, and inexperience. Combat revealed doctrinal problems within the army relating to new technology, particularly tanks and tank destroyers, and identified serious shortcomings in the American replacement system. During 1943–44, the American military worked strenuously to rectify these deficiencies.

For the German defenders, extensive preparations to thwart the invasion began even later. During 1943 the German High Command continued to believe that the Allies were neither materially nor psychologically ready to launch the Second Front. The Germans therefore only modestly enhanced their Atlantic Wall defenses, the allegedly formidable fortifications along the Atlantic coast. Unfortunately for the Germans, the Atlantic Wall existed only adjacent to the major ports; otherwise it remained largely a fiction of Nazi propaganda.

Instead, the German Army in the West – the *Westheer* – remained a backwater of the Nazi war effort. Its primary mission remained supporting the ongoing (and increasingly disastrous) war on the Eastern Front. Throughout 1943 the Germans continued to use France to rehabilitate formations shattered in the east and to work up new divisions to operational readiness, prior to deployment to the Soviet Union and, from September 1943, also to Italy.

The permanent German occupation forces in France thus comprised second-rate coastal defense divisions of limited manpower, firepower, and mobility. Almost no significant operational reserve existed in the west, besides refitting or newly forming mechanized formations. German naval power likewise consisted primarily of numerous small coastal vessels that were incapable of turning back a major invasion force. Moreover, the few German aircraft deployed in the west remained fully preoccupied trying to thwart the Allied air onslaught on the cities and economic infrastructure of Germany. Thus the German military in 1943 was incapable of stopping the Allies if they invaded. Yet, this unsatisfactory position reflected German awareness that the Allies were not yet ready to invade, even if they had wanted to.

This situation changed during November 1943 when Hitler recognized the inevitability of an Allied invasion attempt during 1944 and switched Germany's strategic priority to the west. Over the next seven months there materialized a massive influx of veterans and new recruits as well as Germany's latest and most lethal weapons. The result would be a metamorphosis of German combat power in the west.

By June 1944 the Germans had built up sufficient strength potentially to thwart an invasion: if, that is, they gained some advance warning of where and when the enemy was going to strike, so that they could launch a concentrated counteroffensive to throw the Allies back into the sea. Yet success also required that the German air force and navy at least disrupt Allied mastery of the seas and the skies. The gravest German weakness, however, remained its woefully inadequate logistical base, which, exacerbated by the Allied aerial interdiction campaign, ensured that the Germans lacked the supply stockpiles to win a protracted battle of attrition.

From D-Day to victory

On D-Day, 6 June 1944, six Allied infantry divisions, heavily reinforced with artillery and armor, and supported by a massive air umbrella and naval gunfire, landed astride five invasion beaches. American troops assaulted 'Utah' beach on the southern tip of the Cotentin peninsula and at 'Omaha' along the western Calvados coast. Anglo-Canadian troops landed on 'Gold,' 'Juno,' and 'Sword' beaches between Arromanches and Ouistreham in front of Caen. In addition, the Allies dropped one British and two American airborne divisions along both flanks of the invasion to disrupt German counterattacks aimed at rolling up the beachheads.

The Allied forces experienced contrasting fates on D-Day. Anglo-Canadian forces firmly established themselves ashore on their three assault beaches, but failed to achieve the ambitious goal of capturing the key city of Caen. Although the invaders breached the bulk of the defenses, the Germans held the Pèriers Ridge and prevented the linking up of the 'Gold' and 'Sword' beachheads. Along the ridge that afternoon elements of the 21st Panzer Division counterattacked and successfully pushed through to the coast. But outnumbered and with both flanks unsecured, the Germans retired to the ridge after dark. Moreover, the landing of the British 6th Airborne Division east of the Orne protected the vulnerable left flank of the landing against a weak armored counterattack that the Germans launched that day.

For American forces, the invasion did not go quite as smoothly. At 'Utah' beach, Americans troops quickly established a solid beachhead; however, at 'Omaha' beach, the landing came close to being repulsed. The difficult terrain of steep bluffs bisected by narrow ravines, the loss of most of the amphibious assault armor in rough seas, and the failure of the aerial bombing attacks left the initial assault waves pinned down by murderous German defensive fire. Ultimately, sheer numbers, toughness and heroism, backed by short-range naval gunfire, overwhelmed the defenders and allowed American forces to establish a shallow enclave ashore.

Reflecting the inherent hazard of airborne operations, the drop of the American 82nd and 101st Airborne Divisions inland behind 'Utah' beach and astride the Merderet River became highly scattered and casualties were heavy. The dispersion did have one inadvertent benefit, however, for it confused the Germans as to the real location of the invasion. Though widely scattered, the paratroopers dislocated German communications and prevented a major counterattack against 'Utah' beach on D-Day, allowing the landing troops to establish a firm foothold ashore.

Other factors contributed to Allied success. The absence of many senior German commanders at a war game in Brittany and the disruption of communications due to aerial and naval bombardment both hampered German countermeasures. As significantly, Allied domination of the skies prevented the Luftwaffe from effectively impeding the invasion. The German navy proved equally unable to resist the vast invasion armada. In sum, months of meticulous preparation combined with personal heroism, massive air and naval support, and the achievement of surprise, brought success on D-Day. By the end of 6 June 1944, though few recognized it at the time, the Allies had established a permanent foothold in France.

D-Day, 6 June 1944

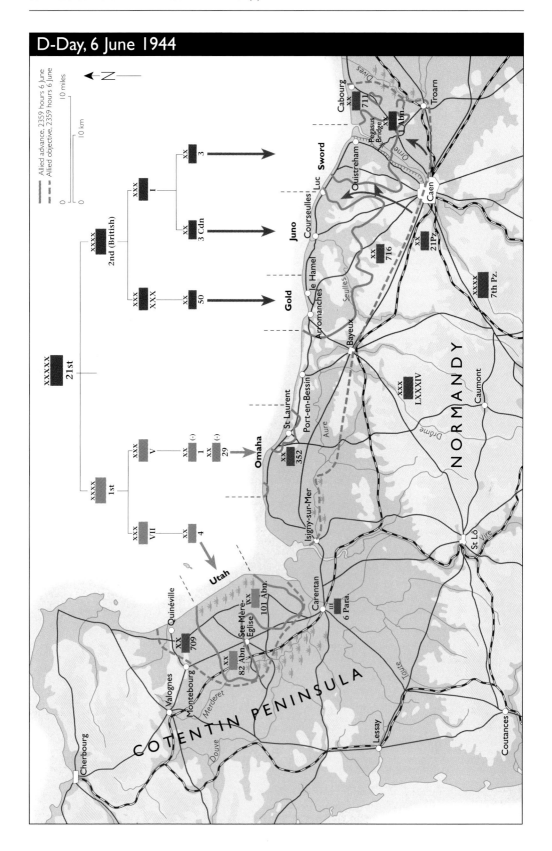

The aftermath of D-Day

After D-Day, little went according to plan. Montgomery's advance quickly stalled when powerful German armored reserves converged on Caen to smash the Anglo-Canadian beachhead. While his forces repulsed these counterattacks, his forces could not gain ground and the struggle for Caen degenerated into a grim six-week attritional battle. Hitler and his commanders believed that the outcome of the campaign hinged on holding Caen, so the Germans massed their best formations opposite the British sector. The narrow bridgehead gave the Germans a relatively short front, allowing them to develop defenses in depth that presented Montgomery with a considerable challenge. Meanwhile, they rushed the II SS Panzer Corps from the Eastern Front for a counteroffensive to smash the bridgehead. In the interim, the Germans stubbornly defended Caen to deny Anglo-Canadian forces room to maneuver.

Neither did American operations go according to plan after D-Day. The Germans temporarily checked the advance of General 'Lightning' Joe Collins' VII Corps from 'Utah' beach toward the key port of Cherbourg along the Quineville Ridge. The advance of Major-General Leonard Gerow's V US Corps on St Lô from 'Omaha' beach was likewise slow. After Isigny fell on 9 June, the way to St Lô stood open, but American caution allowed German reserves to move up and build a new defensive front. Moreover, the priority accorded to Collins' advance on Cherbourg hindered the drive on St Lô. Consequently, the V Corps offensive abruptly ground to a halt 2 miles (3.2km) short of St Lô on 18 June.

The slow advance on Cherbourg forced Collins to abandon the planned direct advance on the port. Instead, on 15 June, VII Corps struck west and cut the peninsula two days later, isolating Cherbourg. Only then, on 22 June, did Collins launch an

Operation Goodwood remains one of the most controversial offensives of the Normandy campaign. Although the abortive British attack to secure Caen and the Bourguébus Ridge suffered very high tank losses, it did facilitate the success of the subsequent American Cobra offensive in the west of the Normandy theater. (NARA)

all-out three-division attack on the port. Though the attenuated defenders fought fiercely, final resistance ceased on 1 July. Although the Americans had finally captured their much-needed major harbor, they had done so well behind schedule and the enemy had left the port in ruins.

On 26 June, along the eastern flank, Montgomery launched his first major offensive, Operation Epsom. It was an ambitious attack to breach the strong enemy defenses west of Caen, force the Orne and Odon rivers, gain the high ground southwest of the city and thereby outflank it. The VIII Corps of Lieutenant-General Miles Dempsey's Second (British) Army spearheaded the offensive backed by strong air, naval, and artillery support. Yet bad luck dogged Epsom: unseasonably bad weather forced Montgomery to attack without the planned air bombardment and the neighboring XXX Corps failed to take the

flanking Rauray Ridge, which hindered the entire attack.

Significant concentration of force finally allowed the British infantry to penetrate the thin German defenses and establish a bridgehead across the Odon River. Thereafter, the 11th Armored Division pushed through and captured Hill 112 beyond. By 28 June, Montgomery had torn a 5-mile (8km) gap in the German defenses. But the methodical advance prevented Montgomery from achieving further gains.

Next, after German reserves had counterattacked the narrow British corridor and the shallow Odon bridgehead, the cautious Montgomery abandoned Hill 112

In order to avoid high casualties, Montgomery favored the use of massive aerial and artillery firepower to support his ground offensives. The effect on urban centers such as Caen, shown here, was devastating. (Imperial War Museum, B7754)

and retired to a shorter, more defensible line. Subsequently, between 29 June and 2 July, VIII Corps repulsed strong, if poorly coordinated, German attacks that constituted the long-anticipated enemy counteroffensive. The newly arrived II SS Panzer Corps hurled itself against the British Odon bridgehead, but made little headway in the face of tremendous Allied defensive artillery fire, and the operation soon fizzled out.

The German counterattack failed primarily because the Germans only had supplies for a few days of sustained offensive action and because they had attacked prematurely with new troops unfamiliar with Normandy's combat conditions. The counteroffensive's failure proved unequivocally that the Allied lodgment had become permanent. Therefore, Hitler devised a new strategy: an unyielding defense to corral the Allies into a narrow bridgehead

and deny them the room and favorable terrain for mobile operations. This decision committed the Germans to an attritional battle within range of the Allied fleet; it was a battle they could not win.

However, Montgomery had neither broken through nor gained the high ground over the Odon in Epsom. It was not until 8 July that he launched a new multi-corps attack on Caen, designated Charnwood. Montgomery again relied heavily on air power to shatter enemy resistance. A strategic bomber raid destroyed several Orne bridges and sharply reduced the Germans'

The Allies' employment of massive aerial and artillery firepower inflicted considerable damage onthe defending Germans. However, the extensive cratering such tactics caused also hampered Allied attempts to advance deep through the enemy's defensive position. (Imperial War Museum CL 838)

ability to resupply their forces in the northern part of the city. Meanwhile, Anglo-Canadian forces launched concentric attacks on the beleaguered and greatly outnumbered defenders. Inexorably, superior numbers and firepower drove the enemy back, and on 9 July Montgomery's troops finally fought their way into northern Caen, four weeks behind schedule. However, Montgomery's exhausted forces were unable to push across the defensible Orne River barrier onto the open Falaise Plain beyond.

Despite reinforcement by Collins' VII Corps, and fresh divisions from Britain, General Omar Bradley's First US Army still struggled to advance in the *bocage* hedgerows when it renewed its offensive toward St Lô on 3 July. Major-General Troy Middleton's fresh VIII US Corps struck south from the base of the Cotentin peninsula with three divisions and in five days took La Haye-du-Puits against stiff resistance. But ferocious opposition stopped the offensive at the Ay and Seves rivers on 15 July. Simultaneously, VII Corps attacked from Carentan toward Pèriers on 3 July, but quickly stalled due to poor weather and difficult marshy terrain. Even after the veteran 4th Division joined the attack on 5 July, VII Corps gained only 750 yards (700m) in four days. The Germans both defended skillfully and counterattacked repeatedly to sap American strength. Though it beat off these counterattacks during 10–12 July, VII Corps had to go over to defense on 15 July.

Gradually, however, American forces solved the problems of hedgerow fighting with improved tactics, enhanced firepower, and better coordination, all of which speeded the fall of St Lô. Major-General Charles Corlett's newly arrived XIX US Corps struck south with three divisions on 7 July to capture St Jean-de-Daye. Thereafter, the corps slowly, but inexorably, gained ground until it cut the Pèriers–St Lô highway on 20 July. The 29th US Division, after renewing its drive toward St Lô on 11 July, both seized the ridge that dominated the northeastern approaches to the city, and advanced across the St Lô–Bayeux highway. On 18 July, the hard-pressed Germans abandoned the city.

American forces had grimly fought their way forward into more open ground and were therefore in a position to prepare a major breakthrough operation, codenamed Cobra.

While the Americans prepared for Cobra, Montgomery launched a major new offensive, named Goodwood, around Caen. This would become the campaign's most controversial operation. In this attack, Montgomery sought to capture both southern Caen and the Bourguébus Ridge – objectives that opened the way to the Falaise Plain to their south. A new attack was necessary to hold German reserves at Caen while the Americans prepared for their break-out bid. However, Montgomery required massive fire support to breach the strong German defenses behind the Orne and it was thus only on 18 July that he attacked out of the bridgehead east of the Orne, which his airborne troops had captured on D-Day. Unfortunately, this bridgehead was so constricted that it proved impossible to preserve surprise and therefore Montgomery had to rely heavily on air bombardment.

Goodwood was both ill-conceived and ill-executed. Aerial bombing and artillery fire enabled British armor to crash through the forward German defenses to the foot of the high ground south of Caen. But the outnumbered Germans nevertheless conducted a delaying withdrawal that disrupted and dispersed the British advance. Thus, British armor reached the Bourguébus Ridge late on 18 July with little infantry and no artillery support. The German gun line of heavy antitank and antiaircraft guns emplaced on the high ground then repulsed the British tanks, inflicting heavy losses. As dusk approached, German combined-arms counterattacks drove the British armor back with further heavy loss.

Montgomery attacked for two more days, but the advance had lost its momentum. Nowhere had his forces established a solid foothold on the vital Bourguébus Ridge, and the heavy losses suffered eroded British fighting power. In fact, the employment of massed armor against intact defenses brought catastrophic tank losses during Goodwood: more than one-third of British

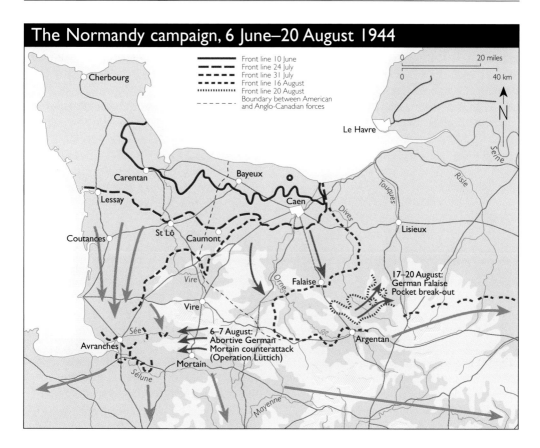

The Normandy campaign, 6 June–20 August 1944

tank strength in Normandy. Moreover, the
offensive failed to 'write down' enemy armor
as Montgomery had intended. Though
Goodwood did gain more ground and
temporarily pinned some German reserves
on the Caen front, these limited
achievements were bought at a price that
British forces could not afford to repeat.

The Cobra break-out

Goodwood nevertheless helped the American
break-out bid by diverting badly needed
supplies from the St Lô sector to the Caen
front to replenish German forces after their
heavy expenditures resisting Montgomery's
attack. The result was serious erosion of the
German logistic position on the American
front prior to Cobra, which facilitated the
American break-out. Allied air attacks had
continually hampered German resupply
operations, thus creating serious logistic

problems. This situation worsened, particularly
on the western sector, after 15 July with the
renewed destruction of the rail bridge at Tours,
the German Seventh Army's major supply
artery. Its supplies thus dwindled on the St Lô
front in the lead-up to Cobra. In fact, the
defending German LXXXIV Corps had less
than two days' fuel left. Thus for the first time
in the campaign, during Cobra supply
shortages crippled the German defenses and
prevented them from cordoning off the
American break-in during 25–26 July, as they
had all previous Allied offensives.

Innovation also aided the American
success in Cobra. To provide the firepower it
lacked, First US Army relied first on carpet
bombing to smash a hole in the German
front; second, on a narrow front offensive to
penetrate the German line; and lastly, on
mobility and speed to outmaneuver, rather
than outfight, the enemy. Bradley, thus,
planned Cobra as a concentrated break-in
attack by three infantry divisions on a

narrow front, supported by intense air and artillery attack, to secure the flanks; meanwhile, three mechanized divisions would punch through to the rear, capture Coutances, and cut off the German LXXXIV Corps on the coast.

The preparatory carpet-bombing was the largest and most effective air attack on ground forces yet seen in the war. While faulty planning, sloppy execution, and bad luck dogged the aerial bombardment, it nevertheless crippled German communications and battered the forward-concentrated Panzer *Lehr* Division so much that even its seasoned troops could not resist VII Corps' concentrated attack. Consequently, the Americans advanced 2 miles (3.2km) into the German defenses on 25 July and, subsequently, American speed and mobility turned this break-in into a break-out. During this exploitation phase, American forces reinforced their success faster than the Germans could redeploy reserves, as mounting logistic deficiencies for the first time crippled the enemy's defense. On 26 July, VII Corps gained 5 miles (8km) as the stretched German front began to collapse.

In response, the Germans rushed the XLVII Panzer Corps (2nd and 116th Panzer Divisions) from the British front to take the American breakthrough in the flank and nip off the penetration. But the American XIX Corps' flanking push south from St Lô disrupted the planned German counterattack and forced the Germans to strike hastily amid the thick *bocage* southeast of St Lô. Both the difficult terrain and mounting supply shortages frustrated the German counterattack, as the panzer forces experienced the same offensive difficulties that had earlier bedeviled American operations. The XLVII Panzer Corps proved unable to hold the ground taken: all it achieved was to build a defensive front facing west and await promised reinforcements.

On 27 July the Americans achieved a decisive breakthrough. As the enemy evacuated Lessay and Pèriers to rebuild a cohesive defense, VII US Corps advanced 12 miles (19km) until it halted just short of Coutances. The next day, the corps captured Coutances and linked up with VII Corps. SS Colonel-General Paul Hausser, the German Seventh Army commander, then erred when he ordered LXXXIV Corps to fight its way southeast in an effort to regain a continuous front, instead of retiring unopposed due south to re-establish a new line south of Coutances. The retiring German forces thus ran into the American spearheads southeast of Coutances and were isolated in the Roncey pocket. With the German front torn open, Bradley expanded Cobra on 29 July. VII and VIII Corps renewed their drive to the south and the next day crossed the River Sienne, took Avranches, and seized a bridgehead across the Sée River, before crossing the Sélune River at Pontaubault on 31 July to open the gateway to Brittany.

Montgomery also resumed the offensive in late July, hastily launching Operation Bluecoat, against the weakly held German front astride Caumont. This rapidly devised attack was intended to maintain pressure on the Germans and prevent the transfer of enemy armor against the Americans. Six divisions of VIII and XXX British Corps assaulted a single German infantry division, but the premature start meant that the attack lacked the massive artillery support that habitually accompanied British offensives. Moreover, though the German defense was weak, the front had been static since mid-June and the Germans had entrenched in depth amid the thick *bocage*.

Initially, British forces quickly penetrated the enemy lines and drew into battle German armor transferring to the American front. Yet, failure to take the flanking high ground at Amaye seriously hampered progress. Caution also prevented British forces from tearing open a barely coherent German front that was ripe to be shattered. On 30 July, the British captured a bridgehead over the River Souleuvre on the undefended boundary between Seventh Army and Panzer Group West. For the next week the two German commands remained detached along this boundary, leaving a 2-mile (3.2km) gap that the British failed to exploit. By the time the British had realized the weakness of the enemy and advanced, German reserves had closed the gap.

The position of the Allied boundary line also hindered a rapid British capture of Vire, imposing a delay that aided the enemy's retreat. The town's quick fall would have severed the enemy's lateral communications lines and seriously hampered the German withdrawal. While the 11th Armored Division of VIII Corps advanced steadily, XXX Corps' armor soon lagged behind, leaving the 11th Armored dangerously exposed as German resistance stiffened on 1 August with the arrival of armor from Caen. On 6 August, German counterblows almost overran the 11th Armored Division's spearhead, but the German armor was keen to push on westward against the Americans and thus launched only limited counterattacks.

American reinforcements move up to Mortain to block the German 'Lüttich' counterattack on 7 August. This operation was one of Hitler's greatest strategic blunders. Unlikely ever to succeed, the operation merely sucked German forces further west into the noose of an encirclement then forming in the Argentan–Falaise area; this ensured that the *Westheer* would suffer a catastrophic strategic defeat in Normandy during August 1944. (US Army)

On 1 August, meanwhile, Bradley's 12th US Army Group became operational and assumed command of the First Army and General George Patton's new Third Army. American forces were now able to conduct the fast-paced mobile war for which the peacetime army had trained. While the First Army advanced southeast and occupied Mortain on 3 August, Patton conducted a spectacular armored advance that first isolated Brittany and then pushed deep into the peninsula to seize Pontivy. Nonetheless, most of the enemy garrison was still able to retire into the ports of Brest, St Malo, and Lorient.

Germany strikes back!

During the break-out, American forces for the first time assumed the defense to thwart a major German counteroffensive that aimed to seal off the American penetration and isolate Patton's command. The American advance had left the center thin, a weakness that Hitler sought to exploit. On 2 August 1944, Hitler condemned the *Westheer* to total defeat when he ordered the new commander of Army Group B, Field Marshal von Kluge, to launch a counteroffensive to retake Avranches and seal off the American break-out from Normandy. This decision was

a strategic blunder that completed the decimation of German forces in Normandy. Although the Germans hastily scraped together the elements of six, albeit much depleted, mechanized divisions, and built up supplies for a few days of sustained offensive action, this was insufficient for success.

Hans von Funck's XLVII Panzer Corps struck during the night of 6–7 August down the narrow corridor between the Sée and Sélune rivers toward Mortain and Avranches. Nonetheless, his troops were too depleted and tired, and von Funck had attacked prematurely before his forces could survey the ground. Moreover, on 5 August the Americans first detected a German build-up around Mortain, while eleventh-hour 'Ultra' intercept intelligence warned of the enemy attack and allowed Bradley to undertake last-minute efforts to bolster his defenses.

American troops were still thin on the ground, occupied unprepared positions, and remained inexperienced at coordinating defensively. Nonetheless, American forces resolutely defended Hill 317, defying all German efforts to push through Mortain toward Avranches. Thereafter, the rapid arrival of American reserves quickly halted the offensive as Allied fighter-bombers disrupted the German drive through the *bocage* once the skies cleared on 7 August. Indeed, the imbalance of forces was simply too great to allow a restabilization of the front and, logistically, the attack was doomed: the Germans had neither the firepower nor the supplies to recapture and hold Avranches.

The defeat of the Mortain counterattack presented the Allies with a strategic opportunity to encircle and destroy the German forces in Normandy, either in the Argentan–Falaise area or via a larger envelopment along the River Seine. With American forces advancing deep into their rear, the only feasible German strategy was to withdraw behind the Seine. Given the dire supply position and dwindling mobility, heavy losses were inevitable since the Mortain counterattack simply thrust the Germans further into the noose of a pocket forming in the Argentan–Falaise area.

However, as American forces raced east to meet Montgomery's troops pushing south from Caen toward Falaise, they became strung out and short on supplies. Fearing over-extension, friendly-fire casualties, and a successful German break-out amid a deteriorating supply situation, Bradley halted the American advance during 13–18 August, divided his forces and directed V Corps to the Seine, which left neither thrust strong enough to defeat the enemy. The Americans had too little strength either to close the Falaise pocket at Argentan firmly from the south, or to push quickly north up both banks of the Seine after V Corps had established a bridgehead across the river at Mantes-Gassicourt on 19 August. By going for a classic double encirclement, the Allies achieved neither objective.

Sluggish Anglo-Canadian progress contributed to the Allied failure to destroy the Germans in the Falaise pocket in mid-August. Although Crerar's newly operational Canadian First Army attacked south toward Argentan in two hastily organized offensives, Totalize and Tractable after 8 August, a combination of inexperience and stubborn German resistance delayed the fall of Falaise until 16 August. Lack of firm British pressure elsewhere allowed the enemy to conduct an orderly withdrawal from the pocket until 19 August, when Canadian and Polish troops finally closed it. In the interim, 40,000 German troops had escaped.

Montgomery feared that his tired and depleted forces would suffer heavy losses and a possible setback if he tried to stop the desperate but determined enemy from escaping. Instead he, like Eisenhower, looked toward a larger envelopment along the Seine. At the same time, Montgomery underestimated the speed and mobility of the American forces; his refusal to alter the army group boundary to allow the Americans to advance past Argentan and close the pocket from the south contributed to Bradley's decision to halt the American advance on 13 August.

It was therefore not until 16 August that Montgomery launched Operation Kitten, the long-planned advance to the Seine. Now the

Light Alllied vehicles such as the one pictured here, had
relatively modest impact inthe hard-slogging battles of June
and July, but once the German front collapsed in August, and
mobile operations ensued, they came into their own.
(Imperial War Museum, CL838)

On 25 August 1944, Allied troops – spearheaded by a French division – liberated Paris from German occupation. During the previous 48 hours, as the Germans prepared to withdraw from the city, French resistance fighters emerged from their places of hiding and commenced an armed uprising against their oppressors. (AKG Berlin)

Germans faced the prospect of a much larger encirclement on the Seine, as their dwindling mobility, catastrophic supply situation, and mounting demoralization presented the Allies with an opportunity to annihilate the enemy against the river. But after 21 August the Germans pulled off their greatest success of the campaign as they extricated virtually all of their remaining forces in a full-scale, staged withdrawal behind the Seine.

Changing strategic priorities, increasing demands for air support, and poor weather prevented Allied air forces from impeding the German retreat. Moreover, the Allied decision of 18 August to capture the Seine bridges intact then brought an end to direct attacks. The break-out also greatly increased the number of potential ground targets and inevitably dissipated Allied air power. Despite repeated air attacks and a catastrophic fuel situation, the Germans salvaged most of their troops and a surprising amount of equipment. They found no respite, however, as Allied forces rapidly advanced beyond the Seine. During the last week in August, therefore, the *Westheer* conducted a headlong

general withdrawal from France back toward the Belgian and German frontiers, closely pursued by Allied forces.

Continued retreat

During 1–9 September 1944, the *Westheer*'s barely cohesive remnants could only slow the headlong Allied advance through France and Belgium. By 10 September, however, this rapid Allied progress had outstripped a logistic network that had never been expected to support such a rate of advance. Consequently, difficulties in getting petrol, munitions, and rations to the front slowed and then stalled Allied progress on a line that ran from the Belgian coast along the Meuse–Escaut canal to Maastricht, and then south from the German border at Aachen to the Swiss border near Belfort.

Reacting with customary German vigor, the *Westheer* seized this fleeting breathing space to rebuild its shattered cohesion. During 6–12 September, for instance, the improvised Battle Group Chill assembled stragglers and local garrison forces to establish a fragile new defensive crust along the Meuse–Escaut canal. To fill the gap that had emerged in the German front between Antwerp and Neerpelt in Belgium, the High Command dispatched from the Reich part-trained army recruits, naval personnel, and air force ground crew to form General Kurt Student's improvised First

Parachute Army. Surprisingly, these partly trained and poorly equipped scratch units offered determined resistance.

A bitter dispute over both strategy and command had erupted between Eisenhower and Montgomery – the 'broad front versus narrow front' controversy – in late August. On 1 September, as planned before D-Day, Eisenhower – while continuing as Supreme Allied Commander – replaced Montgomery as Land Forces Commander in a theater that now deployed two American army groups in addition to Monty's Anglo-Canadian one. Failing to understand that American public opinion would not tolerate a British commander controlling a theater numerically dominated by the Americans, an insubordinate Montgomery campaigned to be reinstated as Land Forces Commander, or at least to be conceded powers of operational control over neighboring American forces.

Although this dispute did reflect Montgomery's egotism, his main motive was to shape the campaign according to the British army's partisan wishes. He desired that his limited British forces – while avoiding heavy casualties – should contribute significantly to Germany's military defeat, within a wider coalition, to secure Britain a strong voice in the postwar political environment. His coordination of neighboring American forces would allow his 21st Army Group – and thus Britain – to achieve a higher military profile than its limited resources would otherwise permit.

This issue of command was interconnected with a similar dispute over strategy. The politically sensitive Eisenhower wished to advance into Germany on a broad front, a strategy that held together the alliance by avoiding favoritism toward any national contingent. The forceful Montgomery, however, argued that his command – reinforced by American forces – should spearhead a concentrated blow north of the Ardennes against the key German Ruhr industrial zone. Displaying profound ignorance of wider political issues, Montgomery based his strategy on sound tactical logic, his own personality needs, and

Britain's own interests within the wider multinational alliance. These two interlocked disputes rumbled on long into 1945, and soured Anglo-American relations during the rest of the campaign.

The V2

Germany's deployment of the V2 ballistic missile in the west during September 1944 forced Montgomery to launch his Market-Garden offensive to remove this threat. The Germans had begun developing this 'vengeance' weapon back in 1940, and in early September 1944 German units in southwestern Holland fired their first missiles against Britain. Hitler hoped that these strikes would break British morale and serve as retaliation for the devastation that Allied strategic bombing had inflicted on the Reich. By the end of 1944, the Germans had fired 491 V2 missiles against British cities in a futile attempt to break Britain's will to fight.

During late 1944, the Germans employed the V2 missile more effectively, by launching 924 rockets – plus 1,000 V1 flying bombs – against Antwerp's harbor to disrupt the unloading of Allied supplies. Some 302 V-weapons hit the docks, destroying 60 ships and inflicting 15,000 casualties, many of them civilian. This sensible employment forced Montgomery to deploy 490 anti-aircraft guns around Antwerp to counter the V1 threat, though against the supersonic V2 the Allies remained helpless.

By early 1945, however, the deteriorating strategic situation and supply shortages were hampering the Germans' use of the V2. Overall, the strategic impact of this supposed war-winning 'wonder weapon' was hugely disappointing, especially given the enormous resources devoted to its development – ones that Germany could have used more effectively, for example, to produce additional tanks, jet aircraft, submarines and flak guns.

Market-Garden

During early September 1944, Montgomery sought to rebuild Allied momentum, lost due to supply problems, before the *Westheer* recovered its cohesion. He hoped to quickly secure both the enemy's V2 launch sites and an intact bridge over the River Rhine, and to use the latter success to secure from Eisenhower priority in the allocation of supplies for a British-led 'narrow-thrust' against the Ruhr. Consequently, on 17 September, Montgomery initiated Operation Market-Garden, an atypically audacious combined ground and airborne offensive.

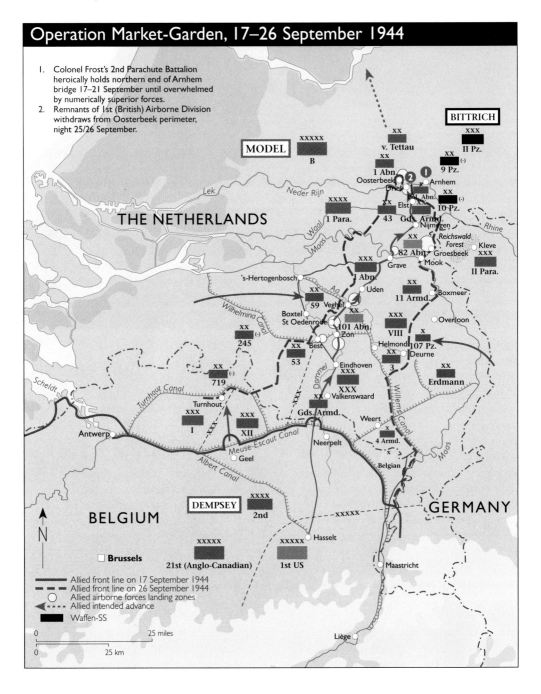

Operation Market-Garden, 17–26 September 1944

1. Colonel Frost's 2nd Parachute Battalion heroically holds northern end of Arnhem bridge 17–21 September until overwhelmed by numerically superior forces.
2. Remnants of 1st (British) Airborne Division withdraws from Oosterbeek perimeter, night 25/26 September.

Allied front line on 17 September 1944
Allied front line on 26 September 1944
Allied airborne forces landing zones
Allied intended advance
Waffen-SS

One motive for this sudden audacity was Montgomery's recognition that early September 1944 offered a fleeting opportunity for the 21st Army Group to achieve his partisan British objectives in the theater. With the *Westheer* brought to its knees, one daring, final, all-out British effort could secure for Britain a high profile within the wider Allied defeat of Germany. If the war dragged on into 1945, however, increasing American numerical domination of the campaign would further erode Britain's declining strategic influence.

Market-Garden envisaged General Brian Horrocks' XXX British Corps thrusting swiftly north through Holland to link up with some 30,000 British and American airborne troops landed at key river bridges and crossroads along the way to facilitate the ground advance. At the northern drop-zone, the British 1st Airborne Division was to seize Arnhem bridge and hold it until Horrocks' armor arrived. The offensive soon encountered difficulties, however, as the desperate defensive improvisations enacted by Field Marshal Walther Model – the new commander of Army Group B – slowed Horrocks' ground advance. To make matters worse, local German counterattacks threatened Horrocks' flanks and even temporarily cut off the flow of supplies to his spearheads. Meanwhile, hastily mobilized garrison forces, stiffened by the remnants of the crack II SS Panzer Corps and reinforced with King Tiger tanks, steadily wore down the heroic resistance offered by Colonel Frost's paratroopers at Arnhem bridge, while simultaneously containing the rest of the 1st Airborne Division in the Oosterbeek perimeter to the west of Arnhem.

After five days' resistance, and without sign of relief by Horrocks' forces, the Germans overran Frost's forces at the bridge. Within a few days, further German pressure had also forced the remnants of the 1st Airborne Division to withdraw from Oosterbeek to the south bank of the lower Rhine. Although Market-Garden was an expensive failure – despite the jusification that Montgomery tried to offer for this operation – the capture of the Waal River bridge at Nijmegen proved strategically vital, for it was from here that Montgomery launched his February 1945 Veritable offensive toward the River Rhine. Moreover, the British commander drew the correct

The distinctive 'Dragon's Teeth' anti-tank obstacles became the characteristic image of Hitler's last fortified position in the west – the Siegfried Line or West Wall. Although the line held up the Allies in places, as well as inflicting heavy casualties upon them, it could not alter Germany's inevitable demise. By early 1945, the Allies had breached the entire Siegfried Line and were pushing the Germans back to the River Rhine. (Imperial War Museum EA 37737)

conclusion from Market-Garden – that even a weakened *Westheer* could still inflict a dangerous reverse on overly ambitious Allied offensive actions.

As Market-Garden was unfolding, Bradley's 12th US Army Group, deployed along the Sittard–Epinal sector, continued its modest eastward progress to initiate the first assaults on the West Wall – the German fortifications along the Reich's western border, known to the Allies as the Siegfried Line. Although supply shortages prevented much of Hodges' First US Army from attacking, the remainder did thrust east to capture Sittard and assault the Siegfried Line near Aachen. Further south, General Patton's Third US Army pushed east 50 miles (80km) to cross the Upper Moselle valley and close on the fortified town of Metz.

Between 13 September and 21 October 1944, it took repeated American assaults to capture Aachen against ferocious German resistance. Protected by the Siegfried Line, the defenders fought tenaciously for this

It took the Americans five weeks of heavy attritional fighting to overcome determined German resistance in the historic city of Aachen: but after its surrender columns of German prisoners streamed west into captivity. (AKG Berlin)

historic city that Hitler had decreed would be held to the last man and bullet. To boost German defensive resilience, military police roamed the rear areas summarily hanging alleged shirkers from trees to encourage the others. Spurred on by such threats and by the need to protect the Reich, the outnumbered defenders resisted vigorously and even launched local counterthrusts against American advances. The few German fighter-bombers available ran the gauntlet of Allied aerial supremacy to strafe the advancing enemy.

Despite these desperate efforts, American determination and numerical superiority eventually told, and on 21 October Aachen fell. The Western Allies had penetrated the much-feared Siegfried Line and captured their first German city. Nevertheless, the considerable time and high casualties incurred in achieving this local success both concerned the Americans and led them to abandon launching individual narrow thrusts against the Siegfried Line.

Clearing the Scheldt

Between mid-September and early November 1944, the First Canadian Army – now temporarily led by Lieutenant-General Guy Simonds in place of the sick General Henry Crerar – struggled to capture the Scheldt estuary in southwestern Holland in the face of fierce enemy resistance. The Germans had managed to establish a solid front in Zeeland – along South Beveland, around Breskens, and on Walcheren island – by extricating the

During 4–6 September 1944, General von Zangen's Fifteenth Army used all manner of vessels – including fishing boats such as these – to mount an improvised evacuation north across the Scheldt estuary to the Breskens area. This successful withdrawal enabled the Germans to hold onto the Scheldt estuary, thus denying the Allies use of the vital port of Antwerp until early November. (Imperial War Museum)

Fifteenth Army from potential encirclement south of the Scheldt estuary. During 4–26 September, this army used improvised boats and rafts to evacuate 86,000 troops and 616 guns north across the estuary.

Most of the Western Allies' supplies were still being landed at the precarious facilities established on Normandy's beaches. This continuing logistic reliance on the original beachheads owed much to Hitler's orders that the German garrisons encircled at French and Belgian ports continue resisting to prevent the Allies from using these harbors. The Allies needed to clear the Scheldt estuary rapidly so that they could land supplies at the port of Antwerp, captured by Horrocks' forces on 4 September. Therefore, between 5 September and 1 October, to secure their rear areas as a prelude to clearing the Scheldt, the

Canadians captured the ports of Le Havre, Boulogne, and Calais.

Unfortunately for the Allies, it took Simonds' understrength army until early November to complete its clearance of the Scheldt. The slow Canadian advance owed much to shortages of resources because Montgomery – despite recognizing the importance of Antwerp's docks – had awarded logistical priority to Dempsey's command for Market-Garden. In addition, the difficult terrain, which assisted a skillful improvised German defense, slowed the Canadians. During 2–16 October, Simonds' forces advanced north to capture Bergen-op-Zoom and seal off the South Beveland peninsula. The German defense here cleverly utilized the terrain, by constructing bunkers in the steep rear slopes of the area's numerous raised dikes, and locating rocket-launchers immediately behind them. The Allies soon learned how hard it was to neutralize these positions.

Meanwhile, between 6 October and 3 November, in Operation Switchback, the Canadians also cleared German resistance in the Breskens pocket south of the Scheldt, after previous Allied attacks in mid-September had been repulsed. Here, the Germans deliberately flooded the Leopold Canal to channel the Canadians onto the area's few raised dike-roads, which the defenders had turned into pre-surveyed killing zones covered by artillery, anti-tank guns, and rocket-launchers. The Canadians had to combine effective artillery support with determination to secure the Breskens pocket in the face of such fierce resistance.

Between 16 October and 1 November 1944, Simonds' forces also advanced west along South Beveland and then prepared to launch an amphibious assault on the German fortress-island of Walcheren. This attack was made possible by an audacious plan – for, at Simonds' insistence, during 3–17 October, five Allied bombing strikes breached the sea-dike that surrounded Walcheren. Through these breaches the sea poured to flood the island's low-lying center,

The culminating point of the First Canadian's Army slogging battles to secure the Scheldt estuary was its assault on the heavily fortified German-held island of Walcheren. To overcome the powerful enemy defenses without incurring heavy casualties, Allied strategic bombers destroyed sections of the island's perimeter dikes, allowing the sea to pour in to flood the low-lying center of the island. (Imperial War Museum C4668)

eliminating 11 of the enemy's 28 artillery batteries. Then, during 1–7 November, in Operation Infatuate, two amphibious assaults backed by a land attack from South Beveland secured the flooded fortress.

Thus, by 7 November the First Canadian Army had successfully cleared the Germans from the Scheldt, but this slogging effort in difficult terrain had cost them 13,000 casualties and had taken no fewer than nine weeks. This sobering experience underscored the Allied high command's belief – derived from the attack on Aachen – that pushing deep into the Reich would prove a difficult task.

During mid-October, while the Scheldt battles raged along Montgomery's western flank, the German forces facing Dempsey's army strengthened their defenses and the British sought to gain better positions for future attacks. Then, out of the blue, during the night of 26/27 October 1944, two German mechanized divisions struck Dempsey's thinly held positions at Meijel, in the Peel marshes southeast of Eindhoven, in a local riposte. Although the Germans initially made progress, Dempsey moved up reinforcements, including massed artillery, and then, between 29 October and 7 November, drove the Germans back to their original positions.

Despite its inevitable failure, the German attack on Meijel demonstrated to the Western Allies that, notwithstanding the disasters that the *Westheer* had suffered in Normandy, it could still mount a surprise counterstrike against weakly defended sections of the Allied line. Equally, though, the riposte also showed the Germans how unlikely such counterattacks were to succeed, once Allied numerical superiority was brought to bear. The initial success of Hitler's surprise mid-December 1944 Ardennes counterattack showed that the Western Allies had not learned the lessons of Meijel; equally, though, the inevitable demise of the Ardennes offensive showed that the Germans had not learned them either.

On 2 November 1944, Eisenhower issued new strategic directives for the campaign. While Devers' and Bradley's commands were to push east to secure bridgeheads over the Rhine in subsidiary actions, Montgomery's army group was to launch the Allied main effort with a strike across the Rhine to surround the Ruhr. As a preliminary to such an offensive, between 14 November and 4 December, Dempsey's army – despite waterlogged conditions – thrust east to clear the west bank of the River Meuse around Venlo. Simultaneously, Simpson's Ninth US Army – now returned to Bradley after serving under Montgomery – and Hodges' First US Army resumed their push through the Siegfried Line toward Jülich and Monschau between 16 November and 15 December.

Although American forces reached the River Roer between Linnich and Düren, VII and V US Corps became locked in bitter fighting in the difficult terrain of the Hürtgen Forest. Unfortunately for Eisenhower, V Corps, in the face of bitter local counter-thrusts, failed to capture the key Schwammenauel Dam that dominated the entire Roer valley. Meanwhile, to protect Simpson's northern flank, the British XXX Corps struck east during 18–22 November to capture Geilenkirchen, before the assault stalled due to saturated ground. This left a German salient that jutted west of the River Roer around

Heinsberg, and Montgomery – who always desired a 'tidy' front line – wanted to clear it before striking further east. But just as British forces prepared to launch Operation Blackcock to secure this area, the German Ardennes counteroffensive erupted.

Further south, on 8 November, Patton's Third US Army resumed its battering assaults on the fortress-city of Metz, but ammunition shortages so hampered these attacks that the town did not fall until 22 November. Elsewhere, Patton's forces – despite continuing supply shortages – made more rapid progress, and by 6 December had secured bridgeheads over the River Roer and penetrated into the Siegfried Line at Saarlautern.

To Patton's south, the offensive initiated by Devers' 6th US Army Group on 13 November made even swifter progress. By 23 November, Lieutenant-General Alexander Patch's Seventh US Army had captured Strasbourg, and over the next 14 days it fanned out to reach the River Rhine on a 50-mile (80km) front. Further south, the seven divisions of General Jean de Lattre de Tassigny's First French Army thrust east through Belfort to reach the River Rhine just north of the German–Swiss border by 20 November. These hard-won advances, which cost Devers' command 28,000 casualties, left a German salient that jutted west beyond the Rhine at Colmar. Yet just as these various Western Allied operations, designed to reach the Rhine and secure bridgeheads over it, neared fruition, the *Westheer* rudely shattered the growing aura of Allied confidence with an unexpected counterblow.

The Battle of the Bulge

As early as 16 September 1944, Hitler had decided to stage a counteroffensive in the west that would seize the strategic initiative and alter decisively the course of the campaign. Hitler hoped to seize the key port of Antwerp by a surprise strike through the Ardennes, despite the unfavorable battlefield situation. Well aware that Allied aerial superiority hampered their mobility, however, the Germans decided to attack only during a predicted period of lengthy bad weather that would ground the powerful Allied tactical air forces.

During October and November the Germans prepared frantically for the attack – now planned to begin in mid-December – while covering their activities with sophisticated deceptions. These preparations included rebuilding the seven shattered panzer divisions slated to spearhead the operation, as well as augmenting German infantry strength with 12 *Volksgrenadier* (People's Infantry) Divisions, recently mobilized by throwing together ex-naval recruits, air force ground crew, and convalescents.

The Germans earmarked the three armies of Model's Army Group B for the offensive, with SS Colonel-General Josef Dietrich's Sixth Panzer Army and General Hasso von Manteuffel's Fifth Panzer Army spearheading the operation in the northern and central sectors, respectively; the weaker Seventh Army was merely to secure the southern flank. Excluding reserves, this force amounted to eight mechanized and 14 infantry divisions with 950 AFVs.

The intended German battle-zone was the hilly, stream-bisected, and forested terrain of the Ardennes, since this region's unsuitability for armored warfare had led the Americans to defend it with just four divisions. Consequently, the Ardennes offered the German attack the prospect of local success, despite its unsuitable terrain. Hitler, however, gambled on an ambitious strategic victory by seeking to capture Antwerp, 95 miles (153km) away, to cut off Montgomery's command from the American forces deployed to his south.

Despite the frenetic German preparations, the attack's objective was too ambitious relative to the modest force assembled and the vast resources on which the Western Allies could call. Indeed, many German commanders argued that their forces were too weak to seize Antwerp, but Hitler remained obdurate. The greatest flaw in the Germans' plan was that their logistical base remained utterly inadequate to support such a grandiose attack. The German forces remained short of fuel, and some commanders planned to utilize captured Allied fuel stocks to sustain the offensive. At Hitler's insistence – and contrary to his senior commanders' professional advice – the *Westheer* risked its last precious armored reserves on the triumph that might be achieved by a barely sustainable surprise blow against this Allied weak spot. Hitler failed to consider the consequences that would accrue if the gamble failed.

The Germans did everything in their power to improve their slim chances of success, with Dietrich, for example, employing his *Volksgrenadier* divisions to conduct the initial break-in, and saving the armor for the exploitation phase deep into the Allied rear. Furthermore, the Germans employed SS-Colonel Otto Skorzeny's commandos – some dressed as American Military Police – to infiltrate behind the Allied lines to spread confusion and help sustain offensive momentum. Although the Germans gained some advantages from this ruse, the operation failed to significantly hamper Allied reactions.

Before dawn on 16 December 1944, the *Volksgrenadiers* of Sixth Panzer Army broke into the Allied defenses before I SS Panzer Corps struck west toward the Meuse bridges south of Liège. SS Lieutenant-Colonel Joachim Peiper's armored battle group spearheaded the corps advance with a mixed force of Panzer IV and Panther tanks, plus 30 lumbering King Tigers that did their best to keep up. Peiper's mission was to exploit ruthlessly any success with a rapid drive toward Antwerp before the Allies could react. Given Peiper's mission and the terrain, his King Tigers played only a minor role in the offensive – contrary to popular perception, which regards this operation as being dominated by these leviathans.

During 18–19 December, Peiper's force stalled at Stoumont because the Americans had destroyed the few available river bridges in the area, and flanking forces had failed to

The Battle of the Bulge, 16–25 December 1944

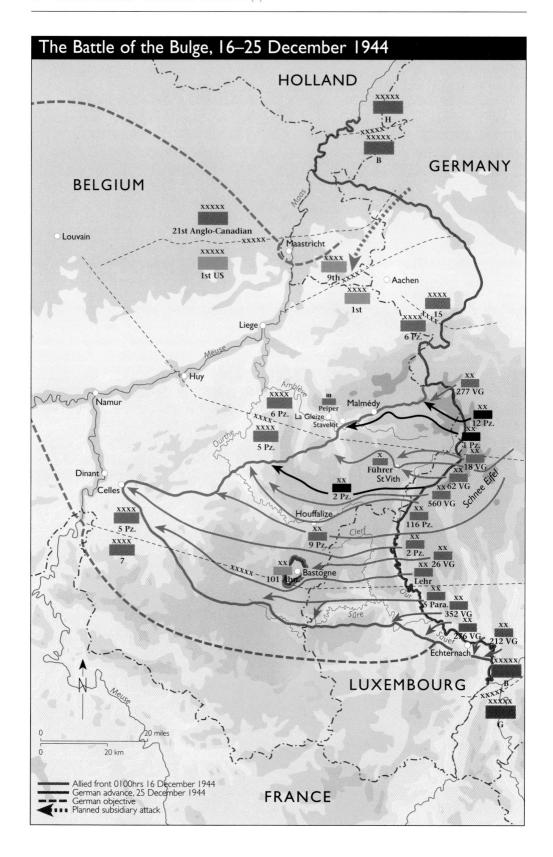

HOLLAND

GERMANY

BELGIUM

H

B

XXXXX

XXXXX
XXXXX

Louvain

XXXXX

21st Anglo-Canadian

XXXXX

Maastricht

XXXX

XXXXX

1st US

9th

Aachen

XXXX

1st

XXXX

XXXX

15

Liege

XXXX

6 Pz.

Maas

Meuse

Huy

XX

277 VG

Ambleve

XXXX

6 Pz.

Peiper

Malmédy

XX

12 Pz.

Namur

XXXX

La Gleize
Stavelot

XX

1 Pz.

5 Pz.

XX

Ourthe

Dinant

Führer

St Vith

XX

18 VG

Celles

XX

2 Pz.

XX

62 VG

Schnee Eifel

XXXX

5 Pz.

Houffalize

560 VG

XXXX

XX

116 Pz.

7

XX

9 Pz.

Clerf

XX

2 Pz.

XX

26 VG

XXXXX

XX

Bastogne

Lehr

XX

101 Abn.

XX

5 Para.

Our

352 VG

XX

XX

Sûre

276 VG

212 VG

Echternach

XXXXX

LUXEMBOURG

B

Meuse

Sauer

XXXXX
XXXXX

G

N

0   20 miles

0   20 km

FRANCE

— Allied front 0100hrs 16 December 1944
— German advance, 25 December 1944
--- German objective
◄··· Planned subsidiary attack

protect Peiper's supply lines. During this advance, Peiper's SS fanatics had murdered 77 American prisoners at Malmédy, plus 120 Belgian civilians in numerous separate incidents. By 22 December, Allied counterstrikes – supported by fighter-bombers after the mist that had kept them grounded over the previous six days lifted – had surrounded Peiper's forces at La Gleize.

During the night of 23–24 December, Peiper's doomed unit – now out of fuel and munitions – destroyed its vehicles, and the remaining 800 unwounded soldiers exfiltrated on foot back to the German lines. The destruction of Peiper's group forced Dietrich on 22 December to commit II SS Panzer Corps to rescue the collapsing northern thrust, but by 26 December this too had stalled near Manhay. Overall, the thrust undertaken by Dietrich's army had proved a costly failure.

On 16 December, to Dietrich's south, the Fifth Panzer Army also struck the unsuspecting Allied front. Although fierce American resistance at St Vith slowed von Manteuffel's infantry thrusts during 16–17 December, further south his two spearhead panzer corps advanced 20 miles (32km) toward Houffalize and Bastogne. During 18–22 December, these corps surrounded the American 101st Airborne Division at Bastogne and pushed further west to within just 4 miles (6.4km) of the vital Meuse bridges. When the Germans invited the commander of the surrounded Bastogne garrison to surrender, he tersely replied: 'Nuts!' After this rebuff the initiative slowly slipped out of the Germans' grasp thanks to fierce American resistance, rapid commitment of substantial Allied reserves, and severe German logistic shortages.

The Americans commenced their counterattacks on 23 December, driving northeast to relieve Bastogne on 26 December, and forcing back the German spearheads near the Meuse. Even though Field Marshal von Rundstedt, Commander-in-Chief West, now concluded that the operation had failed, the Führer nevertheless insisted that one more effort be made to

penetrate the Allied defenses. Consequently, on New Year's Day 1945, von Manteuffel's army initiated new attacks near Bastogne.

To help this last-gasp attempt to snatch success from the jaws of defeat, the *Westheer* initiated a diversionary attack, Operation Northwind, in Alsace-Lorraine on New Year's Eve 1944. The Germans intended that a thrust north from the Colmar pocket – the German-held salient that jutted west over the Rhine into France – would link up at Strasbourg with a six-division attack south from the Saar. Although Hitler hoped that the attack would divert enemy reinforcements away from the Ardennes, in reality Northwind incurred heavy losses, yet only secured modest success and sucked few forces away from 'the Bulge.'

Consequently, the renewed German Ardennes attack soon stalled in the face of increasing Allied strength. Finally, on 3 January 1945, Allied forces struck the northern and southern flanks of the German salient to squeeze it into extinction. Over the next 13 days, instead of immediately retreating, the *Westheer* – at Hitler's insistence – conducted a costly fighting withdrawal back to its original position.

Just one self-inflicted injury marred the strategic triumph secured by the Allies in the Ardennes. As the German advance hampered Bradley's control of the First and Ninth US Armies in his northern sector, Eisenhower acquiesced to Monty's demands and placed these forces under his control. Although the commitment of the British XXX Corps had helped the Allied victory, the Ardennes was essentially an American triumph. Unfortunately, on 7 January 1945, in a press conference Montgomery claimed credit for this victory, thus souring Anglo-American relations for the rest of the campaign.

During the four-week Battle of the Bulge, Model's command lost 120,000 troops and 600 precious AFVs. By mid-January 1945, therefore, only weak German forces now stood between the Allies and a successful advance across the Rhine into the Reich. With hindsight, the Ardennes counterstrike represented one of Hitler's gravest strategic errors. It was a futile, costly, and strategically disastrous gamble that tossed away Germany's last armored reserves. Moreover, the Germans managed to assemble sufficient forces for the counterstrike only by starving the Eastern Front of much-needed reinforcements. Consequently, when the Soviets resumed their offensives in mid-January 1945, they easily smashed through the German front in Poland. By late January, therefore, these German defeats on both the Eastern and Western Fronts ensured that it would only be a matter of months before the Nazi Reich succumbed.

The Western Allies, having by 15 January 1945 restored the mid-December 1944 front line, exploited this success with further offensives. The next day, Dempsey's XII Corps commenced its Blackcock offensive to clear the enemy's salient west of the River Roer around Heinsberg. Hampered both by poor weather, which grounded Allied tactical air power, and by stiff German resistance, XII Corps struggled forward until by 26 January the Allies held a continuous line along the Roer from Roermond down to Schmidt. Then, on 20 January, the First French Army attacked the Colmar salient south of Strasbourg.

The defenders, General Rasp's Nineteenth Army, formed part of the recently raised Army Group Upper Rhine, which was led not by a professional officer but by the Reichsführer-SS, Heinrich Himmler. Unsurprisingly, given Himmler's military inexperience and the losses incurred in Northwind, the French made steady progress, but Hitler equally predictably forbade Rasp from withdrawing. Under pressure, however, Hitler freed Rasp from his chief handicap – he dissolved Himmler's command, subordinated its forces to the more professional control of Army Group G, and brought in the experienced Paul Hausser to lead this command.

Rasp, however, soon realized that these measures could not prevent his forces from being destroyed if they obeyed Hitler's prohibition on retreat. To save his remaining troops, Rasp disobeyed his Führer and withdrew them back across the Rhine, thus saving precious forces with which to defend this last major obstacle before the heart of the Reich. By 9 February, the First French Army held the entire left bank of the upper Rhine.

By early February 1945, the Western Allies were ready to initiate further offensives to secure the remainder of the Rhine's western bank. Hitler, however, now convinced himself that the Allies had temporarily exhausted their offensive power, and so transferred Dietrich's Sixth Panzer Army from the west to the Eastern Front. Yet the Führer did not send this force to Poland, where it was sorely needed to stop the rapidly advancing Soviets, but instead to Hungary for a futile offensive to relieve encircled Budapest.

By now, the Western Allies outnumbered von Rundstedt's three army groups by four to one in manpower and eight to one in armor. In the north, General Johannes Blaskowitz's Army Group H held the front facing Monty's command from Rotterdam through to Roermond, including the vital Reichswald Forest manned by Lieutenant-General Alfred Schlemm's First Parachute Army. Model's Army Group B faced Bradley's forces in the Rhineland from Roermond south to Trier. Finally, Hausser's Army Group G held the front from the Saarland down to the Swiss border against Devers' divisions.

The *Westheer* hoped first to slow the Allied advance through the Siegfried Line, and then gradually retreat back to the Rhine, and there use this obstacle to halt permanently the Allied advance. Hitler, though, again forbade any retreat and insisted that the outnumbered *Westheer* hold the Allies at the Siegfried Line. To retreat back to the Rhine, Hitler argued, would simply transfer the impending catastrophe from one geographical location to another.

On 8 February 1945, Montgomery's forces commenced Operation Veritable, the great offensive for which they had been preparing when the German Ardennes counterattack broke. The reinforced British XXX Corps – now part of Crerar's First Canadian Army –

struck Schlemm's First Parachute Army in its Siegfried Line defenses between Nijmegen and Mook. The offensive sought to drive the Germans back across the Rhine around Wesel to permit a subsequent thrust deep into the Reich. After an intense 1,050-gun artillery bombardment, three British and two Canadian infantry divisions broke into the German defenses. Despite significant Allied numerical superiority, the poor terrain of the Reichswald Forest in the south and the deliberate German flooding of the low-lying Rhine flood-plain in the north, slowed the Canadian advance east.

The Germans also released water from the Schwammenauel Dam to flood the Roer valley on 9 February. This prevented Simpson's Ninth US Army – again temporarily under Monty's command – from initiating its own Grenade offensive toward the Rhine on 10 February. Montgomery intended that Veritable and Grenade would form the northern and southern pincers of a simultaneous double encirclement designed to link up at Wesel on the Rhine. Despite knowing that the flooding had delayed Grenade for 10 days, Montgomery nevertheless continued Veritable after 10 February as planned, because by sucking German reserves to the British thrust, he reasoned, the Ninth US Army would advance more rapidly to Wesel.

Despite penetrating the Siegfried Line, Crerar's forces – now reinforced by II Canadian Corps – made only slow progress. The combination of fierce enemy resistance by newly arrived reserves and the Germans' advantage of defending from their Hochwald Layback defenses, together with poor weather and saturated terrain, all slowed the Allied advance. Nevertheless, Montgomery relentlessly kept the offensive driving east, grinding down the enemy until by 28 February they had been forced back to a small bridgehead west of the Rhine at Wesel. While officially still forbidding any withdrawals, Hitler now realized that the *Westheer* could not hold the Allies west of the Rhine. Consequently, he ordered that any commander who demolished a Rhine

bridge too early – thus preventing retreating German forces from crossing – or who allowed a bridge to fall into enemy hands would be shot. This contradictory order would cause the Germans untold problems on 7 March at Remagen.

Finally, on 23 February, the Americans commenced Grenade across the now subsiding River Roer. As Montgomery expected, these forces made rapid progress toward Wesel as Veritable had already sucked German reserves north, and by 3 March the Americans and British had linked up at Geldern. During 8–10 March, Schlemm – with the connivance of von Blaskowitz – disobeyed Hitler by withdrawing his remaining forces across the Rhine at Wesel before destroying the remaining two bridges. Veritable had cost the 21st Army Group 23,000 casualties in four weeks of bitter, attritional, fighting against the resolute defense that Schlemm had orchestrated. It was only Hitler's grudging acceptance of this fact that allowed Schlemm to avoid execution for his disobedience.

Crossing the Rhine

To the south of Grenade, Hodges' First US Army – part of Bradley's command – commenced an attack across the subsiding River Roer on 23 February 1945 that sought to reach the Rhine between Düsseldorf and Cologne. Meanwhile, Patton's Third US Army thrust toward Trier and the River Kyll, and by 1 March had secured both objectives. After Eisenhower's 3 March strategic directive, Bradley's command expanded these attacks into a drive toward the Rhine between Düsseldorf and Koblenz. By 9 March, the First US Army had reached these objectives and linked up with Simpson's forces near Düsseldorf.

Despite the rapidity of Hodges' advance toward the Rhine, the Germans nevertheless managed to demolish all of the Rhine bridges in this sector – except the Ludendorff railway bridge at Remagen, between Cologne and Koblenz. In a fatal blow to Hitler's

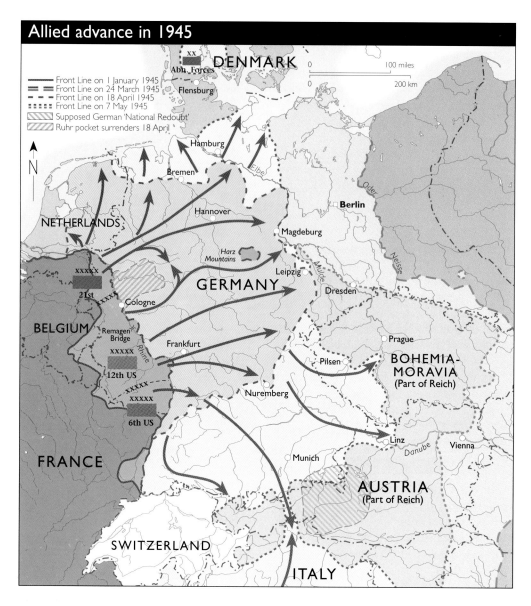

Allied advance in 1945

Front Line on 1 January 1945
Front Line on 24 March 1945
Front Line on 18 April 1945
Front Line on 7 May 1945
Supposed German 'National Redoubt'
Ruhr pocket surrenders 18 April

hopes, on 7 March, Hodges' forces captured the badly damaged – but still intact – Remagen bridge. Recognizing the opportunity that this good fortune offered, Hodges daringly pushed reinforcements across the river to enlarge the bridgehead before the Germans could throw in whatever reserves they had available.

At Remagen on 6 March, with the Americans rapidly approaching the Ludendorff bridge, the garrison commander understandably was anxious. If the enemy captured the bridge, he faced execution; if he blew up the bridge too soon, trapping German forces on the west bank, he faced execution. The commander decided not to blow up the structure until the next morning to allow friendly forces to cross, but unexpectedly American armor – spearheaded by the powerful new Pershing tank – appeared and stormed the bridge. The Germans triggered their demolition charges, which failed to explode, and then ignited the back-up charges, which exploded but only damaged the bridge instead of destroying it. Within hours, substantial

American forces had crossed the river and established a bridgehead on the eastern bank. The elusive intact Rhine bridge had fallen into Patton's hands, and the *Westheer*'s hopes of stopping the Western Allies at the Rhine had been shattered.

Hitler reacted furiously to the loss of the Remagen bridge: he ordered that seven German officers be executed, and sacked von Rundstedt as Commander-in-Chief West. In his place, the Führer appointed Field Marshal Albert Kesselring, transferred from the Italian front. On his arrival, Kesselring mocked the German propaganda that promised the imminent arrival of new war-winning weapons, by stating that he was the long-awaited V3! Predictably, Kesselring's arrival exerted as minimal an impact on the Allied advance as had the two previous German V-weapons. Subsequently, during 8–16 March, as the Americans gradually expanded the Remagen bridgehead, the Germans in vain attempted to destroy the bridge through aerial, V2 rocket, and artillery strikes. The severely damaged bridge eventually collapsed on 17 March, but by then it was too late: Hodges' forces had already constructed several pontoon bridges alongside the now fallen structure.

On 8 March 1945, Eisenhower's new strategic directive confirmed that Montgomery's command would attack across the Rhine near Wesel in Operation Plunder, and issued new orders for both the 12th and 6th US Amy Groups. On that day the XII Corps of Patton's Third US Army had linked up with Hodges' forces in the Remagen–Koblenz area to encircle 50,000 German soldiers north of the Eifel ridge. Eisenhower now instructed Patton's army to drive southeast across the River Moselle into the Saar industrial region toward Mannheim. Here they were to link up with the northeasterly advance of Patch's Seventh US Army, part of Devers' 6th Army Group, through the Siegfried Line from Saarbrücken. The final objective of Patton and Patch's commands was to secure a continuous front along the Rhine from Koblenz to Karlsruhe.

On 9 March, Patton's XII US Corps swung south and, having crossed the Moselle, struck southeast through the Hunsrück mountains toward Bingen on the confluence of the Nahe and Rhine rivers. Then on 13 March, Walker's XX Corps thrust east from Trier through the Saar–Palatinate to link up with XII Corps on the Nahe near Bad Kreuzbach and encircle elements of the German Seventh Army. Last, on 15 March, Patch's Seventh US Army struck northeast from Saarbrücken, aiming to link up with Patton's two corps between Mainz and Mannheim, and to encircle General Förtsch's First Army. As these pincers closed, SS Colonel-General Paul Hausser – recognizing the calamity about to engulf his Army Group G – in vain begged Hitler for permission to withdraw east of the Rhine. By 24 March, Patton and Patch's forces had linked up near Mannheim and successfully surrounded most of Förtsch's disintegrating army. Together these operations inflicted 113,000 casualties on the enemy, including 90,000 prisoners, for the cost of 18,000 American losses.

Then, on 22 March, Patton's forces launched a surprise amphibious assault across the Rhine at Oppenheim, between Mainz and Mannheim, and within 72 hours had established a firm salient east of the river. The Americans now possessed two toeholds across the Rhine, whereas in the north along the supposed Allied main axis, the cautious Montgomery was still readying himself for a massive strike across the river at Wesel. Overall, these hard-fought offensives to clear the west bank of the Rhine, conducted by five Allied armies between 10 February and 23 March 1945, had secured 280,000 German prisoners, for the cost of 96,000 Allied casualties.

Predictably, the Führer reacted to these disasters with increasingly desperate measures to slow the enemy advance. On 19 March, Hitler – in a drastic scorched earth policy – ordered the destruction of anything that the Allies might find of value. By failing to hold back the enemy, Hitler reasoned, the German people had demonstrated their racial weaknesses, and thus had forfeited the right to save their homeland from the cataclysm Hitler now intended to unleash on Germany in a bid to stem the Allied advance. Fortunately for Germany, in the chaos that now pervaded the collapsing Reich, the Minister of War Production, Albert Speer, sabotaged Hitler's intent to plunge the country into an orgy of self-inflicted destruction.

Operation Plunder

During March 1945, as the Americans cleared the Saar–Palatinate and established two bridgeheads east of the Rhine, Montgomery continued building up overwhelming resources for his planned offensive to cross the Rhine around Wesel. The once formidable German First Parachute Army manned this key sector, but its 13 divisions now mustered just 45 tanks and 69,000 weary troops. During the night of 23–24 March, the 21st Army Group – still augmented by Ninth US Army – commenced its attack with massive artillery and aerial strikes. This was followed by an amphibious assault across the Rhine along a 20-mile (32km) front, code-named Plunder, while simultaneously in Varsity two airborne divisions landed behind the German front to shatter its cohesion. The Germans, however, had anticipated an airborne assault and had redeployed many flak guns from the Ruhr, and these downed 105 Allied aircraft.

Despite this, the British had learned from the mistakes made during Market-Garden, and the proximity of the landing zones to the main front ensured that the ground advance linked up with the airborne forces during 24 March. Despite fierce resistance by German paratroopers that delayed XXX British Corps, by dusk on 24 March the Allied bridgehead was already 5 miles (8km) deep. Yet it took another four days' consolidation of the bridgehead before the cautious Monty declared that the struggle for the Rhine had been successful.

By this time, in addition to the Remagen and Oppenheim bridgeheads, Bradley's and Devers' forces had also secured two further crossings of the Rhine. Now, with German units virtually immobilized by lack of fuel and by Allied air power, as well as hampered by chronic equipment shortages, the battered *Westheer* began to disintegrate. To resist the Western Allies' 74 well-equipped divisions, the Germans could now field – even including its Home Guard militia – the equivalent of just 27 full-strength divisions.

After late March, the Western Allies pushed rapidly east beyond the Rhine into the heart of Germany to link up with the westward Soviet advance and thus defeat Hitler's Reich. Prior to 28 March, Eisenhower's strategic intent had been to advance toward Berlin. Yet now, in the final twist of the protracted dispute between him and Montgomery, he shifted the point of main effort to Bradley's planned thrust toward the River Elbe. In so doing, Eisenhower denied Montgomery the glorious, British-dominated, victory the latter so fervently desired.

Then, on 28 March, Dempsey's Second (British) Army broke out from its Rhine bridgehead at Wesel with the intent to clear northern Germany and link up with the Soviets on the Baltic coast near Wismar. Against weak resistance, three British corps made rapid progress and by 8 April had advanced 118 miles (189km) to cross the River Weser southeast of Bremen. Simultaneously, to protect the British left flank, II Canadian Corps struck north from Emmerich and advanced 69 miles (111km) to seize Coevorden in Holland. To slow the British drive east, a desperate Hitler re-appointed his former favorite – the now disgraced General Student – to command the First Parachute Army. Yet by now the strategic situation had so deteriorated that Hitler's arch sycophant – the Armed Forces Chief of Staff Colonel-General Alfred Jodl – could tell his Führer that even the employment of a dozen military geniuses like Student would not prevent Germany's inevitable demise.

During late March 1945, to Monty's south, Bradley commenced attacks to secure

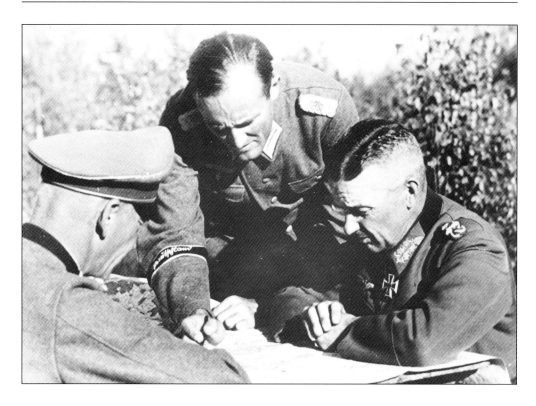

Field Marshal Walther Model, seen here early in the war, was renowned for his iron will. But even this could not save his command from encirclement in the Ruhr pocket during March–April 1945. To avoid being only the second German or Prussian field marshal in history to be captured alive – after Paulus had met this ignominious fate at Stalingrad – Model committed suicide in mid-April after first disbanding his doomed command. (AKG Berlin)

the German Ruhr industrial zone. The Ninth US Army – now returned to Bradley's control – advanced from the Wesel bridgehead along the Ruhr's northern boundary, while the First US Army thrust south of the Ruhr from the Remagen bridgehead. Despite appalling odds, Army Group B commander Model remained determined to fulfil Hitler's orders to stand firm in the Ruhr. This region still delivered two-thirds of Germany's total industrial production, despite the vast damage done by Allied strategic bombing and Germany's belated attempts to decentralize its industrial base.

As the two American armies facing him pushed east, Model guessed that his cautious enemy would swing inwards to clear the Ruhr before driving deeper into the Reich. Consequently, he organized his depleted regular ground forces – now reinforced with Home Guard units and Luftwaffe flak troops – to fight a protracted urban battle for the Ruhr that would inflict the horrific German experience of Stalingrad onto the Americans. The latter recognized the likely heavy costs involved in such an attritional struggle in the ruins of the Ruhr's cities, and instead sought to encircle the region in a deep pocket. On 29 March, however, Model discerned Bradley's intent, and in desperation flung whatever meager reserves he possessed in a local riposte at Paderborn. Despite fanatical resistance, these scratch forces failed to stop the First and Ninth US Armies linking up at Lippstadt on 1 April 1945 to encircle 350,000 troops in the Ruhr – a larger force than that trapped at Stalingrad.

Hitler forbade Model from breaking out and promised a miracle relief operation mounted by the Eleventh and Twelfth Armies, then being raised from Germany's last part-trained recruits as, in sheer desperation, the Germans closed their remaining training schools and flung these troops into the fray. Model, however, remained unimpressed by such Hitlerian fantasies, and so on April 15 – to avoid being the second German field marshal in history to be captured alive (after Paulus at Stalingrad) – Model dissolved his army group and committed suicide. By 18 April, when German resistance in the Ruhr ended, 316,000 troops had entered captivity. The Western Allies had torn a hole right through the center of the Western Front, while to north and south, the *Westheer* was now rapidly disintegrating.

Hitler reacted to the catastrophic setbacks recently suffered on all fronts, as well as to growing signs of defeatism, by increasing the already draconian discipline under which German soldiers toiled. On 2 April, for example, Hitler ordered the summary execution of any soldier who displayed defeatism by advocating surrender or retreat. Even Commander-in-Chief West Kesselring now reminded his soldiers that it was a German soldier's duty to die well. Although these strictures did foster continuing resistance, the main motivation behind such efforts remained the intense professionalism displayed by many German troops – qualities that kept front-line units cohesive despite appalling battlefield losses. Yet now Hitler again displayed his contempt for the army's professional officer corps by placing control of the Home Guard's defense of German cities in the hands of Nazi Party officials, despite the latter's lack of military experience.

In desperation, Hitler committed Germany to a popular 'total war' against the Allies by exhorting the entire population to wage a 'Werewolf' guerrilla struggle in enemy-occupied German territory. Despite extensive propaganda, in reality only a few hundred well-trained Nazi fanatics undertook Werewolf operations, which not surprisingly achieved little. Nazi propaganda also sought to boost German defensive resilience by publicizing the establishment

of a strong defensive position – termed the 'National Redoubt' by the Allies – in the mountains of southeastern Bavaria and western Austria. In reality, this fortified region existed only on paper and when on 22 April Hitler decided to remain in Berlin to face his fate, any inclination to defend this mythical fortress ebbed away. Thankfully for the Allies, there would be no protracted fanatical Nazi last-stand in the mountains, although Allied concern over such a prospect led them to attempt a swift advance through southwestern Germany.

Meanwhile, Patton's Third US Army had broken out of its Rhine bridgeheads during 24–26 March and, in the face of disorganized resistance, had fanned out in rapid thrusts to the northeast, east, and southeast. By 4 May, Patton's forces had pushed 172 miles (275km) across central Germany to capture Chemnitz and Bayreuth. Further south, Patch's Seventh US Army crossed the Rhine at Mannheim and advanced southeast to seize Stuttgart, then Ulm on the River Danube, and finally Nuremberg on 19 April. Simultaneously, the First French Army thrust across the Rhine at Strasbourg and advanced southeast toward Lake Constance. The objective of Patch's and de Lattre's armies was to capture the 'National Redoubt' swiftly before the enemy could consolidate its strength in this region.

Between 9 April and 2 May, the Second (British) Army continued its rapid advance through northern Germany. On 15 April, it liberated the Belsen concentration camp and discovered – as the Americans would do later at Dachau – the heinous crimes that Hitler's regime had committed. Meanwhile, by 19 April, the First Canadian Army had liberated all of northeastern Holland and cut off the remaining German forces in northwestern Holland. The German forces caught in this strategically worthless pocket continued to resist until VE-Day, but largely because the Allies only masked the region and instead focused on more important operations in Germany. Subsequently, during 19–27 April, Dempsey's three corps reached the River Elbe and then – with reinforcements

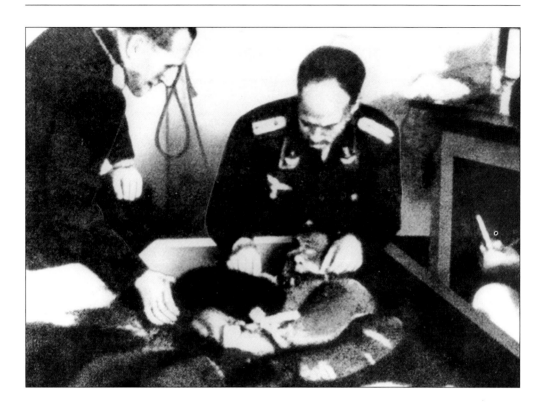

As the Western Allies advanced through the heart of the Reich, the full horrors committed by Hitler's regime became apparent. At Dachau inmates were used as human guinea pigs in experiments conducted by the Nazis. Here, a man is subjected to freezing experiments. (Topham Picturepoint)

from XVIII US Airborne Corps – dashed northeast against light opposition to reach the Baltic Sea at Wismar on 2 May, thus securing Denmark's southern borders just hours before the Red Army arrived.

In the Allied center during 2–19 April, Bradley's divisions struck east, rapidly overrunning central Germany and reaching the Elbe near Magdeburg. Here Eisenhower ordered the Ninth US Army to stop and to wait for the westward Soviet advance to prevent any local confrontations with the Red Army. During the next week, Hodges' First US Army overcame the hedgehog defense mounted by the still-forming German Eleventh Army in the Harz mountains to reach its designated halt-line on the Rivers Elbe and Mulde along a 160-mile (256km) front. Although Hodges' army remained static on the Elbe–Mulde Line during late April, on the 25th an American patrol did push further east to link up with the Red Army at Strehla near Torgau. Between them the Allies had split the Reich in two, an eventuality for which the Germans had prepared by creating a

northern and southern Armed Forces High Command headquarters.

In Bradley's southern sector, on 29 April Patton's reinforced Third US Army commenced the last major American offensive of the war, striking rapidly east and southeast to seize Pilsen in Czechoslovakia and Linz in Austria, respectively. By now the news of Hitler's death had filtered through to German soldiers, and this led many to surrender after only token resistance. Consequently, during 4 May, Patton's forces secured Linz; but just as he prepared to unleash his armor for a dash to Prague, Eisenhower stopped him to avoid any clash with the Soviets.

Meanwhile, further south, Patch's Seventh US Army thrust through the supposed Nazi 'National Redoubt' against only light

resistance during late April. Then, on 1 May, Patch's forces secured the Alpine passes of the Austrian Tyrol, before dashing through the Brenner Pass on 4 May to link up with the Fifth US Army in northern Italy. By then, German resistance had virtually collapsed everywhere except the Eastern Front, and several German commanders in the west – as well as Dönitz's new Nazi regime – had begun to discuss surrender terms with the Allies. The Northwest Europe campaign was now set to enter its final hours.

The final collapse of the Third Reich became imminent once American and Soviet forces linked up with each other at Strehla near Torgau in central Germany on 25 April 1945, thus cutting what remained of the German state in half. The desperate Germans had anticipated such a development, however, and had even created two military authorities – one for the north and one for the south – for the moment when the Allies bisected Germany. (AKG Berlin)

Donald Burgett

Sprinting low to the ground, his feet surrounded by bursts of machine-gun fire, Donald Burgett glanced over his shoulder to glimpse a German Tiger tank lurching toward him. It was 19 December 1944, in a field on the northeastern outskirts of Noville, near Bastogne in the Belgian Ardennes. Intense enemy fire had just set alight the haystack in which Burgett had sought cover, and now the raging flames forced him to dash across the open, snow-covered fields back toward the shelter of nearby houses – a dash that would expose him to deadly enemy fire.

Luckily making it unscathed to a nearby house, Burgett rushed into a room to find two of his squad buddies already hiding there. Looking back through the glassless window frame, however, the paratroopers saw the Tiger approaching the house, and so dashed out of the back door. Within seconds the tank had advanced so that its gun barrel actually pointed through what used to be the front window of the house: then it fired its lethal 88mm cannon. Burgett scarcely avoided the tons of ruined brick that came crashing down on his nearby hiding place as the building's back wall disintegrated. He had survived this close shave, he mused, but for how long could he avoid that lethal enemy bullet 'that had his name marked on it'?

By now a campaign veteran – he had dropped from the skies on D-Day – Burgett realized that the battle at Noville had been his most terrifying combat experience to date. But luckily for historians, Burgett not only survived the campaign, but also wrote down his recollections not long after VE-Day and then published them in a poignant memoir, *Seven Roads to Hell*, during the 1990s.

During the campaign, Burgett served as a private in the 2nd Platoon, A Company, 506th Parachute Infantry Regiment, part of the elite 101st US Airborne Division – the 'Screaming Eagles.' Born in Detroit, Michigan, in April 1926, he volunteered for the paratroopers in April 1943, on the day of his eighteenth birthday, having been previously turned down for being too young. On the night of 5/6 June 1944, he dropped with the rest of the 'Screaming Eagles' behind German lines in the Cotentin peninsula to aid the imminent American D-Day landings on 'Utah' beach. On 13 June he was wounded twice in bitter fighting near Carentan, first by a grenade detonation that left him temporarily deaf, and then by a shell fragment that tore open his left side. After three weeks in hospital, he returned to his division, which soon came out of the front line for much-needed replenishment.

Burgett then dropped with his division around Zon in Holland on 17 September 1944, as part of Montgomery's ambitious Market-Garden offensive. After fighting its way north through Nijmegen, Burgett's company held the front near Arnhem for nine weeks of mostly static actions amid sodden low-lying terrain. Eventually, on 28 November, after 72 days' continuous action, the 'Screaming Eagles' redeployed to northern France for rest and recuperation.

On 17 December 1944, as news filtered through about the success achieved by the surprise German Ardennes counteroffensive, Burgett's division rushed north to help defend the vital road junction at Bastogne. During 19–20 December, Burgett's company resolutely defended Noville against the determined attacks launched by the 2nd Panzer Division. The next day, the Germans outflanked the 506th Regiment, forcing the Americans to conduct a costly withdrawal south through the village of Foy. Over the next week, however, in a series of bitter engagements, Burgett's company

The town of Bastogne represented the key communications node that
General Hasso von Manteuffel's Fifth Panzer Army had to capture so that
it could open up the southern axis of advance in the Battle of the Bulge.
The determined resistance offered by the 101st US Airborne Division
around Bastogne – as demonstrated at Noville during 19–20 December –
ensured that the encircled town never fell into German hands. (US Army)

At Marvie, a village located just to the east of Bastogne, fierce
resistance by American paratroopers helped prevent German
armor from dashing into Bastogne before a defensive perimeter
could be consolidated. When the Germans invited the
surrounded American garrison to surrender, the reply of their
commander was terse: 'Nuts!' (US Army)

helped drive the Germans back to the start lines they had held prior to the commencement of their counterstrike.

Burgett's recollections vividly captured the brutal realities of combat in the Northwest Europe campaign – the diseases that afflicted soldiers, the terrible wounds suffered in battle, the awful food on which they had to subsist, and the intense emotions generated by these experiences. For example, he recalled with horror the diseases that lengthy exposure to Holland's wet conditions caused among the front-line troops. Burgett himself suffered from trench mouth, an ailment that made his gums ooze with pus and left his teeth so loose that he could easily move them with his tongue. Although penicillin eventually cured him, he then succumbed to trench foot after his boots disintegrated due to the length of his continuous front-line service in sodden terrain.

Scabies was another problem from which Burgett's company suffered in Holland, an unpleasant condition where microscopic parasites develop under the skin, causing insatiable itching. Such a disease flourished in the unhygienic conditions in which the paratroopers often served. Indeed, while in the front line near Arnhem, Burgett's comrades only occasionally managed to take what they termed a 'Whore's Bath' – a quick scrub of the head, armpits and crotch with icy cold water collected in their helmets. It was only when the division went on leave in France during late October 1944 that Burgett managed to take his first hot shower in 10 weeks!

Sanitary arrangements, too, were often rudimentary. During the 101st Division's dash north to Bastogne on a bitterly cold 17 December, for example, the 380 open-topped cattle trucks that carried the paratroopers did not stop at all during the 24-hour journey, not even for a quick toilet stop. This meant that those unfortunate soldiers who could not wait any longer had to perform their bodily functions over the back of the truck's tail gate.

Such lack of hygiene, of course, proved a particularly serious problem for those paratroopers unlucky enough to be wounded in battle. Burgett recalled the moment during the savage 19 December battle for Noville when a new replacement soldier suddenly ran into view around the corner of a building, screaming in agony. Enemy fire had caught him in the stomach, and in his arms he carried most of his intestines, the remainder dragging along the ground through the dirt.

It took Burgett and two of his squad to hold down the sobbing soldier so that they could carry out emergency first aid. Laying a tattered raincoat down on the ground, the paratroopers placed the injured man on it and proceeded to wash his entrails, picking out the larger bits of dirt as best they could, before shoving his guts back inside his wide-open abdomen. They then tore the raincoat into strips, bound the man's midriff with this filthy makeshift bandage, and gave him the vital shot of morphine that each soldier carried. Finally, they dragged the wounded private into the relative safety of a nearby ditch while another trooper dashed off in search of a medic – all this being undertaken while enemy artillery rained down on their location. While such desperate measures undoubtedly saved many wounded soldiers' lives, the filthy conditions in which the wounds were either inflicted or initially treated often subsequently led soldiers to succumb to virulent infections.

Apart from the ever-present fear of death or serious injury, the other concern that dominated the paratroopers' lives, Burgett recalled, was food. A soldier's aluminum mess kit – bowl, knife, and fork – was his most important possession next to his weapon. If a soldier lost his mess kit in action, there were seldom any replacements, and the luckless individual had to use his helmet to take his ration from the regimental field kitchen. In tactical situations that allowed soldiers to draw food from the field kitchen, Burgett would always sprint to the front of the queue, then wolf down his food – just on the off-chance that if he rushed to the back of the queue, there might just be enough left over for some meager seconds.

For much of the time at the front, however, the fighting prevented hot food from reaching the troops, and then the soldiers had to subsist on boiling up their dehydrated K-Rations and 'consuming' their D-Bars. The unpopular K-Rations were stodgy, lumpy, and tasteless substances but – as Burgett recollected – if you had not eaten for several days, even K-Rations could taste tolerable. Even more unpopular, however, was the D-Bar, a mouldy-tasting so-called chocolate bar. These were so hard, Burgett maintained, that you could not smash one with your rifle butt, or melt it by boiling! Burgett insisted that he never successfully managed to consume a single bar throughout the campaign.

Apart from fear, disease, discomfort, and hunger, many of the other emotions that Burgett experienced during the campaign stayed with him. He vividly remembered, for instance, the odd little superstitions that some soldiers held. Many paratroopers from America's southern states would never take the first sip out of a liquid container that had a closed lid: as you opened the lid, so the old-wives' tale went, the Devil lurking inside would get you. Burgett also recollected that when a veteran 'Old Sweat' experienced a premonition of his own impending death, very often that individual would be killed by enemy fire in the following days.

Although Burgett himself did not experience any such frightening premonitions, he was well acquainted with the phenomenon of abject terror. He recalled, for example, the sense of mind-numbing fear that overwhelmed him during one phase of the battle for Noville. He lay, heart pounding and sick with nausea, in the bottom of a slit trench just outside the town, while German Panther tanks moved round the American positions, systematically spraying the frozen ground with their machine guns. With no bazookas or satchel charges available, Burgett and his comrades had no choice but to press their bodies into the mud at the bottom of their trenches and pray that the tanks did not come close enough to collapse the trench on top of them. The fear of a horrible death by crushing or suffocation effectively paralyzed him and left him almost unable to breathe. Burgett even remembered that at one point the enemy tanks were so close that he could feel the heat of their engines warming the bitter winter's air.

Perhaps surprisingly, even when the enemy came as close to Burgett as they had at Noville, he merely regarded them as abstract objects – either you killed them first, or else they killed you. Rarely did the enemy individuals whom he faced in close-quarter combat register as human beings in his mind for more than a few hours. Usually, the immediate requirements of staying alive and accomplishing the mission took priority over any sense of compassion for his opponents.

One particular German soldier, however, stayed in Burgett's mind long after the war had ended. The incident occurred in late December 1944, as the paratroopers drove the Germans back to the positions that they had held before the Ardennes counteroffensive commenced. In a dense wood, Burgett came across a wounded, and obviously helpless, enemy soldier. As Burgett contemplated what to do, one of his comrades stepped up and shot the German dead. Burgett exploded in anger, grabbed his comrade, and threatened to blow his brains out if he ever again shot a German who was attempting to surrender. For the rest of the campaign, in quiet moments between engagements, the imploring face of this anonymous enemy soldier would return to haunt Burgett's thoughts.

Few sources reveal the often-unpleasant realities that ordinary soldiers faced in war better than a soldier's memoirs written close to the events. This certainly remains true of Donald Burgett's recollections. Whether it be the strange superstitions, the unpleasant rations, or the heroism of emergency first aid dispensed to a wounded comrade while under enemy fire, any study of the Northwest Europe campaign is enriched by drawing on such vivid memories of those individuals who participated in its events.

Rationing and retaliation

The Northwest Europe campaign exerted an influence on the nations involved in these operations that extended far beyond the battlefield. It impacted on both the international and domestic politics of the states prosecuting the campaign, as well as influencing powerfully their economies, societal fabrics, ethical attitudes, and cultural heritage. First, Anglo-American cooperation during the campaign cemented the transatlantic alliance between them and ensured that their 'special relationship' flourished during the postwar period. In addition, the military necessity that underpinned the campaign dramatically increased cross-cultural interaction between the two nations, yet simultaneously generated cultural friction.

Inevitably, a proportion of the large numbers of American personnel stationed in the United Kingdom during 1943–45 formed relationships with British women; consequently, some British women became 'GI Brides,' and a generation of children were born to Anglo-American parents. The presence of American troops created friction with their male British counterparts because of their complaints about warm British beer, because of the luxuries they enjoyed, which few 'Brits' had seen for years, and because of their success in attracting attention from British women. Underpinning this friction were mutual cultural ignorance, misunderstanding, and prejudice on the part of both peoples.

One area where this necessity of military cooperation exposed divergent cultural perspectives was the issue of race. The

American armed forces remained segregated into 'white' and 'colored' units and naturally they sought to continue this segregation

In Central Germany on 8 May 1945 – Victory in Europe Day (VE-Day) – American soldiers met up with troops from the Red Army to celebrate their defeat of Hitler's heinous Nazi German Reich. (AKG Berlin)

when deployed overseas in the United Kingdom and on the continent of Europe. But this attempt to export American racial segregation to the United Kingdom encountered considerable opposition from the British government and people, whose sense of fairness and solidarity with anyone fighting Nazi oppression, irrespective of their nationality, creed, or religion, was offended by such overt discrimination.

While the war strengthened ties between Britain and America, it accelerated the loosening of the bonds of the British Empire, including the Dominions as well as Britain's colonies. The Canadians, for example, were determined, for reasons of national pride, to retain the autonomy of the First Canadian Army throughout the Northwest Europe campaign; in contrast, the British War Office adopted a rather condescending attitude that

sought to keep Canadian troops under overall British military control. This tension dominated the professional relationship of Montgomery and Canadian General Henry Crerar during the 1944–45 campaign.

Thus operations in this theater tended to aggravate the already growing Canadian perception that their British 'masters' could not avoid displaying an oppressive, imperialistic paternalism toward them. In the postwar era, this development increased the mounting domestic Canadian sentiment for full independence, a process that culminated in the 1982 Constitution Act's removal of the last vestiges of British authority over Canada.

The Northwest Europe campaign also changed domestic politics among the combatants. Nazi Germany had long been a one-party totalitarian dictatorship, so the campaign in this sense had little impact on German domestic politics. Yet the setbacks that the Wehrmacht experienced in Normandy did embolden the anti-Hitler resistance movement. This fostered the attempt to assassinate Adolf Hitler with a bomb positioned at the Führer's headquarters at Rastenburg in East Prussia on 20 July 1944, an attack that only narrowly failed. The Nazi state responded viciously to this attempted assassination, arresting, torturing, and executing in particularly gruesome ways the leading conspirators.

On the Allied side, Britain had formed a government of national unity early in the war and domestic partisan politics were largely, though not totally, subordinated to the greater needs of the war effort. In contrast, within the United States, domestic politics continued as usual. The Republicans, always more isolationist in outlook, used the war to mount partisan attacks against President Roosevelt's Democratic presidency and his continuation of New Deal policies.

The campaign exerted a more marked impact on Canadian domestic politics. The need to provide more manpower for the theater provoked a domestic political crisis in Canada during 1944. In the first phase of the war, the Canadian government could

only send volunteers to serve overseas. Then, in 1942 the Canadian people passed a referendum allowing the government to dispatch overseas conscripts called up under the National Resources Mobilization Act (NRMA) of 1941. Unfortunately, francophone Quebec continued its traditional hostility toward the pro-British Canadian government and voted overwhelmingly against the referendum.

Fearful of exercising the authority conferred upon it by the people, the Canadian government prevaricated and refrained from dispatching conscripts to northwest Europe long after they were desperately needed. The Prime Minister, Mackenzie King, hoped that the war would end before he would have to exercise such controversial authority. But the heavy Canadian casualties suffered at Falaise, as well as in clearing the Channel ports and the Scheldt, left the Canadians significantly deficient in combat troops.

Reluctantly, therefore, in November 1944 the Canadian government decided to send the 'Zombies' (as Canada's volunteer soldiers derisively dubbed the conscripts) to northwest Europe. They arrived tardily and in the face of considerable opposition both domestically and from the 'Zombies' themselves. In fact, extremely serious absence without leave and desertion problems emerged among the 'Zombies' soon after they arrived in northwest Europe and few saw extensive combat service.

Economically, the Second World War brought material deprivation for the civilians of all the protagonists. The Northwest Europe campaign was no exception. Every nation resorted to varying degrees of rationing, although the United States, protected by its geographic isolation from the war in Europe, was the least affected by domestic food rationing. Britain, with its maritime lines of communication threatened by U-boat attacks, introduced stringent rationing early and launched a major campaign for self-sufficiency, which produced the allotments that can still occasionally be found even today in British cities and towns.

In the case of Germany, Hitler at first kept rationing to an absolute minimum in order to protect the civilian morale that had collapsed in the latter stages of the Great War. But as the war turned against Germany and defeats in the west added to those in the east and south, rationing became progressively more stringent. Rationing was

One of the chief privations suffered by the British people during the Second World War was stringent rationing of food and goods through the use of the coupon system. With German U-boats attempting to strangle the supply of foodstuffs and manufactured goods arriving into Britain from across the seas, the British government also had to embark on a crusade for agricultural self-sufficiency, and manufacturing. The former was made possible by the creation of thousands of small allotments in urban areas. (ISI) also extensive for French, Belgian, and Dutch civilians until released from German occupation by the Allied advance across northwest Europe. Since the Germans ruthlessly stripped France of resources and productive capacity to support the German war effort, civilians were forced to make do on meager rations.

Subsistence was particularly difficult for the Dutch population cut off in the isolated 'Fortress Netherlands,' in the north of the country, during spring 1945. The Germans had extensively flooded the low-lying land to hamper the Allied advance, but this measure also drowned large areas of farmland. The combination of flooded land, the general wartime dislocation of agricultural and economic production, and large-scale German depredations ensured that in spring 1945 the occupied Netherlands was unable to meet its basic subsistence needs and thus the populace slowly began to starve to death. Indeed, ration quotas sank so low that, in desperation, the German command was forced to allow the Allies to fly in foodstuffs for the civilian population during the last weeks of the war.

Societies in transition

Socially, the Second World War, like all total wars, provided a motor for accelerated social change and a general relaxation of social mores among all the combatants. The departure of so many men to war, the massive relocation of individuals from self-contained rural environments to cities, and the ever-present prospect of death threatened the sanctity of marriage, and saw an explosion of premarital sex and casual sexual encounters. Indeed, the experiences of the war dramatically increased the acceptability of casual sex, and while postwar governments and societies tried hard to restore prewar social values, they were never entirely successful. For soldiers away from wives and sweethearts, military service exposed them to the temptations of

prostitutes, and thus introduced the dangers of venereal diseases.

The four years of German occupation inevitably brought extensive 'fraternization' between French, Belgian, and Dutch women and German soldiers as well. One of the saddest aspects of the Allied liberation of France was the social ostracism and violence directed by both the Resistance (Maquis) and ordinary French civilians against women who had 'fraternized' with the enemy: many of these individuals suffered physical abuse, forcible shaving of their heads, and public humiliation. In fact, the Allied liberation brought a more general vicious settling of scores against alleged collaborators. In the Channel Islands – the only part of the British Isles to fall under Nazi occupation – the issue of collaboration continued to divide this once tightly knit community for several decades after 1945.

These retaliations reflected one particular unfortunate effect of total war on the populations involved: that the experience of violence begets more violence. This, as de Gaulle's regime found in France during 1945, made it difficult to return swiftly to prewar civilian control following the liberation from Nazi occupation.

The war also gave British, American, and Canadian women, at least, dramatically increased opportunities for participation in the war effort. Women served extensively in the defense industries, freeing men for combat duty. They served as auxiliaries at headquarters, in communications, as well as in administrative and medical services. Here they not only made invaluable contributions to the Allied victory, but lived very different lives from those they would have experienced if the war had not erupted. Young women enjoyed much greater independence, paying their own way,

Right. Once the Allies had liberated parts of Nazi-occupied northwest Europe, alleged collaborators found themselves facing harsh summary 'justice.' French women – such as this individual – who had collaborated with the Germans had their hair shaved off and were treated as social outcasts. (AKG Berlin)

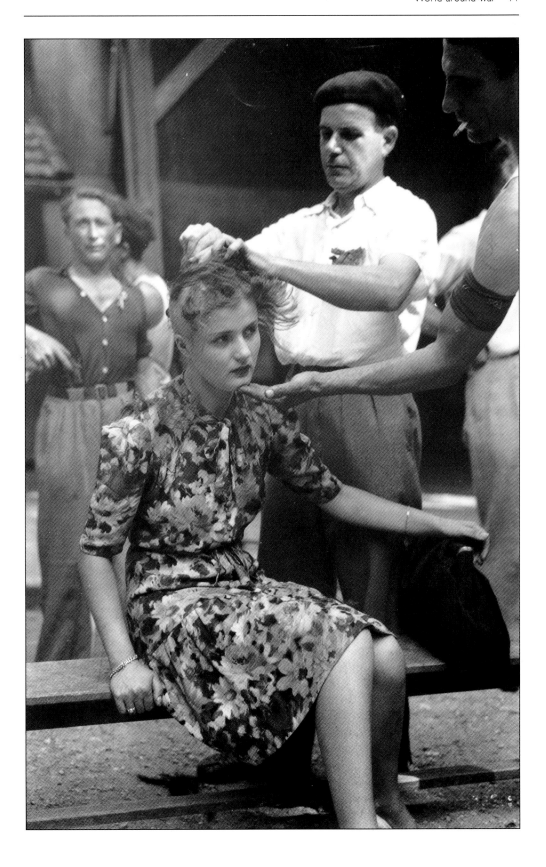

Like most 'total wars,' the harsh demands placed on the state during the 1939–45 war by its need to prosecute the conflict led to rapid social change. British women, for example, worked extensively in the war economy, as well as undertaking auxiliary functions within the armed and public forces, such as manning antiaircraft defenses and fighting fires. (ISI)

working away from family, and being surrounded by like-minded friends.

In contrast, Hitler refused to mobilize women more extensively for the German war effort, and this represented one of Germany's greatest strategic mistakes of the war. Reflecting the traditional, patriarchal gender roles that National Socialism extolled, Hitler saw the principal wartime role of women as simply to produce and nurture a new generation of blond-haired, blue-eyed Aryan Nazi warriors. The Nazi failure to harness its female population more extensively to support the war effort, as did their Allied opponents, contributed directly to the defeat of Nazi Germany in May 1945.

The Second World War was truly a 'total' war. One manifestation of this was the unprecedented mobilization of youth for war. This was particularly true of totalitarian Germany. As the tide of war turned against them, the Germans progressively accepted younger and younger volunteers into the military. These volunteers, who underwent preliminary premilitary training, were drawn from the paramilitary Hitler Youth movement.

In 1943, for example, the Nazis raised the 12th SS Panzer Division Hitler Youth, consisting of 17–18-year-old volunteers, and the division distinguished itself repeatedly during the northwest Europe campaign. So young were these soldiers that they were not allowed the standard armed forces cigarette ration, instead receiving boiled sweets! Despite their youth, or perhaps because of it, they proved some of the most fanatical Nazi soldiers, having endured years of intensive ideological indoctrination and propaganda. This fanaticism manifested itself in the fields of Normandy in war crimes, in which Hitler Youth Division soldiers murdered Canadian troops who had surrendered.

Combatant or civilian?

Another dimension of both the Second World War and the 1944–45 campaign as total conflicts was the increasing blurring of the distinction between civilians and combatants, and the resultant increasing 'collateral' damage suffered by civilian populations. This was particularly true of the air war. Buoyed by the strategic bombing theorists' misguided mantra that air power could single-handedly win the war by

destroying the morale of the German civilian population, the Western Allies launched massed attacks by heavy bombers on German industrial and urban targets.

While RAF Bomber Command attacked German cities at night, the United States Army Air Force pursued daylight precision attacks against centers of German industry. The result was the deaths of hundreds of thousands of German civilians and the diversion of massive German resources into passive and active countermeasures, including static antiaircraft artillery batteries, searchlights, early warning radar, bomb shelters, and rescue services, as well as day and night fighters.

For German civilians the last two years of the war were a story of increasing terror as Allied aircraft launched attacks of increasing intensity and lethality. They culminated in the Dresden bombing of February 1945, where casualties were not that far below those suffered in the subsequent atomic bomb drops on

During 1944–45, as Germany's battlefield situation deteriorated further, an increasingly desperate regime began to draft younger and younger Hitler Youth teenagers into the armed services to replace the vast casualties suffered on all three fronts. The German Home Guard Militia (*Volkssturm*) comprised young boys, pensioners, the infirm, and essential war workers previously exempted from military service. (ISI)

Hiroshima and Nagasaki. For the Allied air crews carrying out these missions, their task proved to be one of the most dangerous military occupations of the Second World War. Despite the prewar claims that the bombers 'would always get through,' often they did not, and thousands were shot

down and their crews killed, maimed, or taken prisoner.

During spring 1944 the Allies turned their fleets of heavy bombers toward France and began an interdiction campaign intended to isolate the Normandy invasion site. The Allies bombed bridges, railway stations, and marshalling yards, particularly along the Seine and Loire rivers. So intensive were these attacks that by D-Day the Allies had destroyed every major rail bridge into Normandy and the Loire and Seine rivers, isolating the Normandy battlefield. At the same time, however, so as not to give away

The prolonged Allied strategic bombing campaign against Germany inflicted appalling damage on buildings and caused heavy civilian casualties. Despite this, the campaign failed – in contradiction to the ideas of the interwar theorists – to break the will of Germany's populace to continue the war. (IWM B7754)

the invasion site, the Allied bombers had to deliberately dissipate their attacks to disguise the location of the actual invasion, striking targets of opportunity all across northern and western France.

While this bombing campaign did achieve its aim of crippling France's communications and hampering German redeployment and movement, unfortunately it also inflicted thousands of casualties on French civilians. This was particularly true of the novel carpet bombing attacks, in which heavy bombers were used in direct support of ground forces on the battlefield. First tried at Monte Cassino in Italy during spring 1944, this was a very complex and inherently hazardous

application of air power. It required great precision, depended heavily on technology for its accuracy, yet was subject to human error. It therefore had mixed success. One of the most tragic incidents of unintended 'collateral damage' was the 7 July 1944 raid on Caen, which killed more than 700 French civilians and flattened much of the medieval part of the town. The raid barely scratched the German defenders deployed on the city's northern perimeter.

Another new feature of the Second World War was the development of rockets capable of hitting both military and civilian targets over long distances. The Germans responded to the Allied D-Day landings in Normandy by initiating their V1 'Vengeance' rocket attacks on London, beginning on 10 June 1944. Because the V1 lacked accuracy and Hitler thirsted to avenge the Allied strategic bombing campaign, the Führer launched these rockets at the civilian population of southern England. These 'Buzz Bombs,' as the British dubbed them, proved difficult to intercept and shoot down, and could rain indiscriminate havoc down on British towns.

However, such attacks failed to break British civilian morale – just as the German bombing 'Blitz' of 1940 had failed to do. In fact, deploying the V1 represented an unproductive diversion of precious Nazi resources. Though they did require considerable Allied resources to counter them, they were wrongly targeted at civilians. Instead, Hitler should have employed them against the Allied invasion fleet and Normandy bridgehead, where they could have hampered and disrupted Allied military operations.

The supersonic, jet-propelled V2 missile that the Germans unleashed during autumn 1944 proved more damaging. The Germans employed this deadlier missile to better effect, directing many of their strikes against the crucial port of Antwerp, through which flowed the bulk of Allied supplies for the entire northwest Europe theater. For the Belgian citizens of Antwerp this was a terrifying manifestation of total war that was very difficult to stop, and it caused considerable civilian loss of life.

Another situation in which innocent civilians became unwitting victims of war in northwest Europe was the reprisal policy that the Germans implemented in retaliation for sabotage and assassination attacks by the Resistance. The German occupying forces frequently executed 10 civilians for every German soldier killed or wounded in such strikes. The most egregious massacres occurred after D-Day as heightened levels of Maquis attacks threatened the German lines of communication within rural France.

The worst German reprisal atrocity occurred at Oradour-sur-Glane on 10 June. Here, troops of the 2nd SS Panzer Division *Das Reich*, in addition to carrying out many summary executions, herded the bulk of the village's population into the church and set it alight. In total, the Germans murdered 642 innocent French civilians in reprisal for the death of just one of its officers in a Maquis ambush.

Similarly, thousands of French Resistance fighters captured by the Germans both prior to and during the northwest Europe campaign were tortured and executed by the occupiers, including the famous French social historian Marc Bloch. In addition, as the prospect of liberation loomed large, Allied forces having established themselves in Normandy after D-Day, a particularly vicious cycle of assassination and reprisal emerged between the Maquis and pro-Nazi French collaborationist paramilitary organizations such as the *Milice*.

The Nazi Holocaust

The Germans compelled thousands of French, Belgian, and Dutch men to 'volunteer' for labor service within the Reich, where they were poorly treated, overworked, and subject to high fatality and injury rates through industrial accidents. The Germans, of course, also deported 'racial and political' enemies to both forced labor and concentration camps. During their occupation of France, the Germans, aided by French anti-Semites, rounded up and deported the bulk of the country's prewar Jewish population. Most of France's Jews – some 77,300 individuals – met a grisly death in Nazi concentration and extermination camps, together with 129,000 Dutch and Belgian Jews. Those who tried to shelter deportees also risked deportation or execution themselves.

In fact, the Nazi 'New Order' in France encouraged the latent racism and anti-Semitism ingrained in sections of western society to flourish anew. In France, the Netherlands, and Belgium, pro-fascist parties and movements often eagerly cooperated with the Nazis in identifying, rounding up, and deporting Jews and other racial enemies of the Reich. Such political organizations hoped to be allowed to govern their home countries under benevolent Nazi stewardship once Germany had won the war. The latter's defeat in 1945 probably obscured the fact that the Nazis had little inclination

The railway spur inside Birkenau, looking back toward the main gate. Birkenau was the labor camp attached to Auschwitz, the most infamous of the Nazi extermination camps, where Hitler's minions enacted their heinous 'Final Solution of the Jewish problem' – the extermination of 5.5 million of Europe's Jews. (AKG Berlin)

to permit the sort of autonomy aspired to by these local fascist parties.

Censorship was widely enacted by all the combatants during the Second World War. In Nazi Germany and its occupied territories it was near total. One important resistance activity was to publish clandestine 'free' presses, while millions of people in German-occupied Europe daily risked arrest and deportation to listen on the radio to the BBC Overseas Service for developments in the war. Even among the Western Allied powers fighting to free occupied Europe from Nazi oppression, wartime necessity compelled the suspension of many normal civil rights. Under the slogan 'careless talk cost lives,' extensive restrictions were placed on the freedom of the press.

Such restrictions reached their height during the preparations for Operation Overlord, the D-Day landings. Those few privileged individuals in the know as to the date and location of the invasion were allocated an extra top-secret security clearance designated 'Bigot.' Pre-invasion paranoia led to some unfortunate detentions.

One individual was arrested for publicly calling another man, who by coincidence possessed a 'Bigot' security clearance, a bigot. Though he was talking about the individual's narrowed-minded, prejudiced views, fears of a security leak led to his arrest! Another unfortunate victim was a national crossword designer who inadvertently included a number of the codenames for the D-Day landing beaches in a crossword. For fear that he was a Nazi spy communicating clandestinely with his bosses, he was arrested and detained until after the invasion had taken place.

The 1944–45 campaign, as well as the wider Second World War, did considerable damage to European culture. The Nazis, no lovers of diversity anyway, seized enormous quantities of artwork and forms of cultural expression from the states of northwest Europe; many of these pieces were never seen again after 1945 and of those that did emerge, only a small proportion were ever returned to their rightful owners. With their narrow, traditional artistic tastes, the Nazis labeled many manifestations of the avant-garde, progressive art that flourished during the anxiety-laden interwar era as 'degenerate.' This, of course, included any expressions of Jewish, Gypsy (Roma), or African-American culture and heritage.

Western architecture suffered significant damage due to both the extensive ground operations conducted in northwest Europe during 1944–45 and the protracted Allied strategic bombing campaign. Some of the most famous architectural monuments of western Europe, including the German cathedrals of Cologne and Aachen, as well as Notre Dame in Paris and St Paul's in London, all suffered varying degrees of damage that necessitated extensive postwar reconstruction.

The gravest cultural damage inflicted during the Second World War, however, was the Holocaust: the Nazis' genocide against the Jews of Europe. In what constituted one of the worst crimes committed in history, Hitler's regime came perilously close to successfully eradicating Jewish culture in Europe. Only the combined success of the Western Allied campaigns in northwest Europe and Italy, and the Soviet advance from the east, ensured that Hitler's Reich was defeated in May 1945 before this heinous mission was completed.

Many of Europe's most impressive architectural sites suffered extensive damage during the 1939–45 war, due either to ground fighting or to aerial bombing. This image depicts St Paul's Cathedral surrounded by fires after a Luftwaffe bombing attack on London during the 'Blitz' of 1940. (Ann Ronan Picture Library)

Brenda McBryde

The campaign proved just as crucial an experience for the non-combatants involved in the theater as for those soldiers who served in the front line. One such non-combatant was nurse Brenda McBryde, who was born just 10 days before the armistice ended the First World War. During 1938, Brenda started a four-year course of nursing training at the Royal Victoria Infirmary, Newcastle upon Tyne. In April 1943 she qualified as a state registered nurse and then was commissioned into the British army as a nursing officer in the Queen Alexandra's Imperial Military Nursing Service (Reserve). After seven months' service with the 75th British General Hospital at Peebles in Scotland, Brenda moved with this unit to Sussex in preparation for commitment to France once the Western Allies' Second Front had commenced. Within a fortnight of D-Day, the 75th had redeployed to the village of Rys in Normandy, close to the coastal town of Arromanches.

During her nursing service in northwest Europe, Brenda encountered some grisly sights in the field hospital, but years of professional training helped her to take these experiences in her stride. The most depressing duty that Brenda faced, she recalled, was working in the head injuries ward. A large proportion of these soldiers had lapsed into comas, and these patients Brenda had to feed with milk, egg, and glucose inserted through a nasal tube. The biggest problems for such patients, Brenda recollected, was that their permanently half-open mouths would become infected during that summer's hot humid weather. In the absence of eating that produced saliva to cleanse the mouth, the coma victims' mouths soon became encrusted with pus, and so Brenda had to cleanse their gums with antiseptic many times each day. Sadly, only a few of the patients ever woke from their comas.

When deployed in Normandy, the 75th also treated injured enemy soldiers who had been captured. Brenda's experiences in treating enemy troops enabled her to form distinct – if stereotypical – impressions of the German soldier's character. Her hospital only received large numbers of enemy wounded during the rapid Allied advance of August 1944, forcing it to create entire wards just for enemy prisoners, and these wards soon took on national characteristics. The wounded Germans, Brenda noticed, soon became distressed by the lack of rules as to what was or was not permitted on the ward. Within an hour of the creation of the first exclusively German ward, the enemy patients had appointed a duty officer, whom Brenda derogatorily addressed as the 'Tent-Meister.' This individual would shout 'Achtung!' every time a nurse entered the ward, and all the conscious patients, lying on their beds, would click their heels together in response. But the formidable hospital matron soon put a stop to this nonsense: 'We'll have none of your nasty Nazi habits here,' she said in her best commanding voice, as she brusquely turned over the nearest German patient and enthusiastically rammed a penicillin needle into the hapless individual's buttocks!

Brenda soon realized, however, that most of the wounded Germans, who increasingly were young lads and old men, were little different from her wounded Allied patients. Indeed, on one occasion, a moving incident occurred that shed much poignancy on the absurdity of war. One morning a young German began to sing the popular soldier's song 'Lili Marlene,' and when the nurses failed to hush him down, the rest of his convalescing comrades joined in. Next, from the adjacent ward, British patients began to sing the same song – in English instead of German – until an enthusiastic but good-natured competition developed between them. Brenda recalled that this display of spontaneous high spirits broke the gloom that continually hung over the wards.

Some German patients, however, proved to be very different from the rest of their comrades. On one occasion, for example, Brenda treated a barely conscious German trooper who had lost one leg; he was clearly identifiable as a member of the elite Waffen-SS by his silver and black collar runes. As she fed the patient a glass of water, the soldier came to his senses, opened his eyes and instinctively smiled at the individual who was tending to him. Within seconds, however, after his vision had focused on Brenda's uniform, his grateful demeanor suddenly changed. With a convulsive jerk, the SS-trooper spat into her face and screeched, with whatever venom he could muster, a string of obscenities at her. Brenda's commanding officer had witnessed the incident and in a voice hard with anger, he instructed the staff not to treat the SS soldier until all the other newly arrived cases had been dealt with. That was the only time in Normandy that Brenda recalled a German patient being treated differently from a British one: irrespective of nationality, patients were treated in strict order according to the severity of their injuries.

During her service in northwest Europe, Brenda also encountered the discomforts that even noncombatants had to face during wartime. For seven weeks in Normandy, for example, she went without a hot bath, making do with a quick rinse every morning and night with cold water carried in a large biscuit tin. Then, in early August, the nurses heard of a French convent near Bayeaux where you could get a hot bath for just a few francs. So one morning, when she had a rare spell of off-duty time not consumed with sleep induced by exhaustion, Brenda and two of her fellow nurses went on a bathing trip. They arranged a lift in a borrowed jeep, and arrived at the convent only to find a large queue at the entrance: obviously, good news traveled fast in times of adversity. Carrying – like everyone else in the queue – a rolled-up towel and a modest piece of soap, all three waited patiently in line for their turn. When they got to the head of

the queue, Brenda paid the sister a few francs and entered the tiny whitewashed hut. Inside, Brenda undressed and slipped into the deep copper bath, filled with steaming hot water. What bliss!

When all three nurses had finished this luxurious experience, they topped it with another treat that had been denied them for months – a drink at a coffeehouse. Admittedly, the 'coffee' was just an ersatz brew made from ground acorns that tasted like stewed boots. But despite this, Brenda found that just being able to relax and view the world around her for a few minutes was in itself a luxury after an incessant seven-week cycle of tending patients, bolting down unappetizing food, sleeping, and then resuming her duties.

As Brenda worked in a field hospital deployed close to the front line, she also faced the hardship of limited availability of food. The only hot beverage available was 'Compo Tea,' an insipid drink made from a cube of dehydrated tea, milk and sugar. It was usually 'brewed' in a large bucket and carried around the wards for staff and patients alike. The nurses often had to use biscuit tins to drink this unappetizing concoction due to a shortage of mugs. Food remained quite restricted, and this proved a problem for those patients who required a high-protein diet.

Brenda hit on the idea of trading with the local French population. The nurses held a 30-minute outpatients' clinic every morning to treat the local population's minor injuries; after treatment, the nurses in return went round with their tin helmets to collect eggs and other farm produce. When the hospital's commanding officer heard about this unofficial activity, he simply made sure he was on the other side of the camp every time the outpatients' clinic took place, so that he never publicly 'discovered' this sensible yet unauthorized arrangement.

These hardships became noticeably more intense in mid-July, when Brenda's commanding officer sent her and a colleague on temporary duty to a field dressing station just behind the front line. This proved necessary because storms had delayed the evacuation of wounded personnel back to

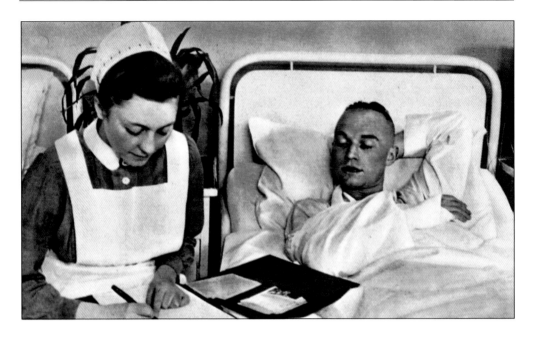

Britain and, consequently, a backlog of patients had emerged at their first point of call, the front-line dressing stations. As this was a combat zone, the conditions were rudimentary indeed. The nurses slept on camp beds in a 3ft-deep (1m) trench that was roofed over with wooden planks and a canvas tent. Their latrine was simply a tent erected over a large pit in the ground. Every night, the exhausted nurses' sleep was disturbed by the ground-shaking effect of sustained artillery fire.

Understandably, the station commandant was concerned that the arrival of two nursing officers might have a marked impact on the platoon of engineers deployed to help construct its facilities. Consequently, he ordered that an official painted sign bearing the message, 'Sisters' Quarters – Keep Out!' be erected outside the nurses' new 'home.' With typical soldiers' humor, within 24 hours a crudely painted sign had appeared outside the engineers' canvas-covered trenches, bearing the rejoinder, 'Brothers' Quarters – Come In!'

Despite the commandant's efforts, the nurses nevertheless unwittingly caused quite a stir among the engineers. Once a week the nurses had their 'bath night.' They would stand under their tent – naked except for their tin hats – with each foot in a biscuit tin of cold water, and wash themselves down. It was only

Nurses working in field hospitals in both the UK and active combat theaters also faced some risk from enemy aerial bombing, in addition to the normal stresses associated with wartime nursing service. That said, the War Office believed that the presence of female nursing sisters in forward areas did provide a powerful boost to the morale of wounded soldiers. (AKG Berlin)

as they left the dressing station that one engineer confessed to them the interest that bath night had generated among the soldiers. The glare of the nurses' lamp meant that their illuminated silhouettes could be seen on the tent's canvas sides. After the word had got around, once a week the engineers would silently creep down toward the nurses' quarters to watch with fascination the latest performance of 'bath night'!

These few incidents should make it clear that the campaign proved a pivotal experience for a young and, up to that point, relatively sheltered nurse such as Brenda McBryde. Noncombatants, as well as the front-line soldiers, clearly encountered real challenges in this campaign. Whether this was a distressing encounter with an ungrateful Nazi fanatic, or the touching experience of a spontaneous singing competition, or even the despair of treating coma patients with little chance of recovery, Brenda certainly saw a lot of life in her few months spent in northwest Europe.

The road to VE Day

The key event that made possible the end of the Northwest Europe campaign – and the entire Second World War in Europe – occurred at 3.30 pm on 30 April 1945. At that moment, the German Führer, Adolf Hitler, committed suicide in the Reichschancellory Bunker in Berlin, as above ground triumphant Soviet forces advanced to within 330yds (300m) of this installation. Back on 22 April, as Soviet spearheads began to encircle the German capital, Hitler had abandoned his notion of escaping to lead Germany's war from Berchtesgaden in Bavaria, and instead decided to remain in Berlin to meet his fate.

Even into the last hours of his life, Hitler remained determined that Germany would continue its desperate resistance against the Allied advance, if necessary to the last man and round, irrespective of the destruction that this would inflict on the German nation. With the Führer's death, so passed away this iron resolve to prosecute to the last a war that almost every German now recognized as already lost. On 30 April, though, Hitler ordered that, once he had taken his own life, Grand Admiral Karl Dönitz, Commander-in-Chief of the Navy, should replace him as Führer. His successor, Hitler instructed, was to continue Germany's resistance to the Allies for as long as possible, irrespective of the cost.

A view of the entrance to the Reichschancellory Bunker near which Hitler's corpse was burned after his suicide on the afternoon of 30 April 1945. With his death, the Nazi leadership could now abandon Hitler's futile – and ultimately self-destructive – mantra of resistance to the last bullet. (AKG Berlin)

Yet even before the Führer's suicide, it seemed to him that several rats had already attempted to desert the sinking Nazi ship. On 23 April, for example, Hitler's designated deputy, Reichsmarschall Hermann Göring, had informed Hitler – now surrounded in Berlin, but very much alive – that as the latter had lost his freedom of action, the Reichsmarschall would assume the office of Führer. An enraged Hitler, interpreting this as treason, relieved Göring of his offices and ordered his arrest.

The day before, Reichsführer-SS Heinrich Himmler had secretly met Count Folke Bernadotte of Sweden at Lübeck. At this meeting, Himmler offered to surrender all German armies facing the Western Allies, allowing the latter to advance east to prevent more German territory falling to the Soviets. The Reichsführer hoped that his offer would entice the Western Allies into continuing the war that Germany had waged since 1941 against the Soviet Union – the common enemy of all the states of Europe, Himmler believed. The Western Allies, however, remained committed to accept nothing other than Germany's simultaneous unconditional surrender to the four major Allied powers. Moreover, they recognized Himmler's diplomatic approach as nothing more than a crude attempt to split their alliance with the Soviets, and so rejected Himmler's offer on 27 April. When Hitler heard of Himmler's treachery on 28 April, he ordered that his erstwhile 'Loyal Heinrich' be arrested.

Simultaneously, and with Himmler's connivance, SS Colonel-General Karl Wolff, the German military governor of northern Italy, continued the secret negotiations that he had initiated with the Western Allies in February 1945 over the surrender of the German forces deployed in Italy. On 29 April – the day before Hitler's suicide – in another vain attempt to split the Allied alliance, a representative of General von Vietinghoff signed the instrument of surrender for the German forces located in Italy. By 2 May,

During the period 1–23 May 1945, Admiral Karl Dönitz acted as Nazi Germany's Second Führer after Hitler's Last Testament named him as his successor. On 23 May, however, the British arrested Dönitz and his cabinet at their Flensburg headquarters near the German–Danish border. Subsequently, Dönitz was tried by the Nuremberg Tribunal and sentenced to 10 years' imprisonment. (Imperial War Museum HU 3011)

some 300,000 German troops in this area had already laid down their arms.

On 1 May 1945, the new Führer, Karl Dönitz, established his headquarters at Flensburg near the German–Danish border in Schleswig-Holstein. Dönitz immediately abandoned Hitler's futile mantra of offering resistance to the last bullet, and accepted that the war was lost. Instead, Dönitz attempted merely to continue the war to save what could reasonably be rescued from the Soviets' grasp. By surrendering German forces piecemeal in the west, Dönitz hoped that the Western Allies would occupy most of the Reich to spare the bulk of the German nation from the horrors of Soviet occupation.

Furthermore, when the advancing Western Allies neared the rear lines of the German forces still locked in bitter resistance against the Soviets in the east, Dönitz hoped to withdraw these troops – plus the isolated garrisons of East Prussia and Courland – into Western Allied captivity. In this fashion, Dönitz hoped to save the bulk of the German army in the east from the nightmare of years of forced labor in Stalin's infamous prison camps.

But during 1–2 May 1945, Germany's already dire strategic situation deteriorated further, undermining Dönitz's strategy of calculated delaying actions. In that period, Montgomery's forces cut off Schleswig-Holstein from Germany by linking up with the Red Army on the Baltic coast, while the Americans consolidated their link-up with the Soviets in central Germany. Although on 3 May the German army could still field over five million troops, it was obvious to all that within a few days the Allies would overrun what little remained of Hitler's supposed Thousand-Year Reich.

Given these harsh realities, on the morning of Thursday 3 May, Dönitz sent a delegation under a flag of truce to Montgomery's new tactical headquarters on the windswept Lüneberg Heath. The delegation wished to negotiate the surrender to Montgomery of not just the German forces that faced the 21st Army Group but also the three German armies of Army Group Vistula then resisting the Soviets in Mecklenburg and Brandenburg.

Montgomery stated that he would accept the surrender of all German forces that faced him in northwestern Germany and Denmark, but could not accept that of those facing the Red Army, who had to surrender to the Soviets. If the Germans did not immediately surrender, Montgomery brutally warned, his forces would continue their attacks until all the German soldiers facing him had been killed. Montgomery's stance shattered the German negotiators' flimsy hopes of securing, at least in this region, a salvation from looming Soviet captivity. Disheartened, they returned to Flensburg to discuss their response with Dönitz and German Armed Forces Commander-in-Chief Field Marshal Wilhelm Keitel.

The Germans arrived back at Montgomery's headquarters on the afternoon of Friday 4 May. At 6.30 pm in an inconspicuous canvas tent, on a standard army table covered with a rough blanket for this momentous occasion, Grand Admiral Hans von Friedeberg signed an instrument of surrender. By this instrument he capitulated to the British the 1.7 million German troops who faced Montgomery's forces in northwestern Germany and Denmark, with effect from 8.00 am on 5 May. In his moment of triumph, a gloating Montgomery entered the wrong date on the historic surrender document, and had to initial his amendment.

After this surrender, the Western Allies still had to resolve the issue of the capitulation of the remaining German forces deployed along the Western Front. During 5 May, and into the next morning, the negotiating German officers dragged their feet to buy time for German units then still fighting the Soviets to retreat west in small groups to enter Western Allied captivity. Meanwhile, on the afternoon of 5 May, General von Blaskowitz surrendered the encircled German forces in northwestern Holland to the Canadian army, while on the next day, the German Army Group G deployed in western Austria capitulated to the Americans.

Then, on 6 May, Colonel-General Alfred Jodl, Chief of the Armed Forces Operations Staff, flew from Flensburg to Supreme Allied Commander Dwight Eisenhower's headquarters at Rheims, where the latter expected him to sign the immediate unconditional surrender of all remaining German forces to the four Allied powers. Initially, Jodl tried to negotiate only the surrender of those German forces still facing west, excluding those on the Eastern Front. In response, Eisenhower threatened to abandon the negotiations and close the Western Front to all Germans soldiers attempting to surrender, unless Jodl immediately agreed to the unconditional surrender of all Germans forces in all theaters. Jodl radioed Dönitz for instructions, and received his reluctant permission to sign. At 2.41 am on 7 May 1945, Jodl signed the instrument of surrender, which was slated to take effect on 8 May at 11.01 pm British Standard Time. The Germans used the remaining 44 hours before the Second World War in Europe officially ended to withdraw as many forces as possible from the east and surrender them to the Western Allies.

Finally, in Berlin at 11.30 pm on 8 May, after the cessation of hostilities deadline had passed, von Friedeberg and Keitel again signed the instrument of surrender concluded at Rheims the previous morning to confirm the laying down of German arms. Officially, the Second World War in Europe was over. Dönitz's government continued to function until 23 May, when it was dissolved and the second Führer arrested. Subsequently, the Nuremberg War Crimes Tribunal sentenced Dönitz to 10 years' imprisonment. Despite the official German surrender on 8 May, though, many German units in the east continued to resist the Soviets during the next few days. Indeed, the very last German forces did not surrender until 15 May 1945, a full week after Germany's official surrender. But by this date, it is fair to say that both the 1944–45 Northwest Europe campaign, and the entire Second World War in Europe, had finally ended.

At 11.30 pm on 8 May 1945 in Berlin, once the deadline for the cessation of hostilities agreed the previous day had passed, Field Marshal Keitel signed the confirmatory German instrument of surrender. The supposed Thousand-Year Nazi Reich had, in fact, lasted only a little over a decade. (AKG Berlin)

'The most devastating and costly war'

On 23 May 1945, 15 days after Germany's unconditional surrender, the Allies dissolved Dönitz's residual government. From that point, the German state, in effect, had ceased to exist, and instead the Western Allies and the Soviets established interim military occupation administrations based on the territory they had liberated by the end of the war. This situation lasted until July when, at the Potsdam International Conference, the 'Big Four' – America, Britain, France, and the Soviet Union – confirmed earlier agreements to establish

four separate occupation zones within a territorially reduced German state. The conference ceded German territory east of the Oder–Neisse River line, plus southern East Prussia, to the re-established Polish state, and the northern part of East Prussia to the Soviet Union. Elsewhere, Germany returned to its 1936 boundaries, which meant the restoration of an independent Austria and the return of Bohemia-Moravia to a reconstituted Czechoslovakia; in addition, the French temporarily acquired the Saar industrial region.

The division of Germany and the emergence of the Cold War in Europe, 1945–57

Berlin: Divided into four national occupation zones 1945–49; West Berlin became part of the German Federal Republic in 1949, despite being entirely within the Soviet-controlled German Democratic Republic.

1. Eupen-Malmédy: Annexed by Germany from Belgium in 1940; returned to Belgium in 1945.
2. Luxembourg: Annexed by Germany in 1940; restored as an independent state in 1945.
3. Saar region of Germany: To France 1945–57.
4. Alsace-Lorraine: Annexed by Germany from France in 1940; returned to France in 1945.

- German Federal Republic from 1949; joined NATO 1955
- Reconstituted Yugoslav state
- Reconstituted Polish state
- Parts of pre-1939 Germany ceded to Poland
- Parts of pre-1939 Germany ceded to Soviet Union
- Warsaw Pact zones

At the Potsdam International Conference in July 1945, the four victorious major Allied powers – 'the Big Four' – agreed the postwar division of Europe. Here Churchill and American President Truman pose for the press. The conference agreed that Germany should return to its pre-1936 boundaries, and be divided temporarily into four national Allied occupation zones. The quadripartite Allied Control Commission in Berlin administered the country. (IWM BN 8944)

This quadripartite Allied administrative division of Germany left the Soviets controlling the country's four eastern provinces (*Länder*), the British administering northern Germany, the French southwestern Germany, and the Americans central and southern Germany. In similar fashion, the four victorious powers also divided the German capital, Berlin – now entirely within Soviet-controlled eastern Germany – into four separate sectors, the Soviet zone being in the east of the city. Berlin housed the Allied Control Commission, the supreme executive power in Germany. The Potsdam Conference also guaranteed access routes from the Western Allied occupation zones into West Berlin by air, road, and rail. Last, the Allies also established four similar occupation zones in a reconstituted Austrian state detached from

Germany. As these cooperative arrangements unfolded, however, the Soviet Union simultaneously began creating Communist satellite regimes in the territories it had liberated, namely Poland, Czechoslovakia, Hungary, Romania, and Bulgaria.

As the four Allied powers began their administration of Germany, they found the country in a ruinous condition. During the last months of the war, seven million Germans had fled from the east to the Reich's western *Länder* to escape the Soviet advance. In the weeks following the German surrender, a further three million either fled or were expelled from Communist-controlled areas into the western occupation zones. These refugees, together with the two million displaced persons already in the three western occupation zones, created a vast administrative burden for the Western Allies. If this was not bad enough, all four Allied powers had also to deal with some nine million former prisoners and slave-laborers then located within the Reich, who required repatriation back to their original countries.

As 50 percent of German housing had been destroyed by May 1945, the Allies had to improvise vast refugee and internment camps to house these displaced persons, plus five million surrendered service personnel. Any German house lucky enough still to possess an intact roof in June 1945, for example, soon came to house several dozen inhabitants in exceedingly cramped conditions, while many families had to live in the cellars of bombed-out dwellings. Not surprisingly, conditions both in these camps and in German towns were often rudimentary, and for most Germans during late 1945 the best they could hope for was to subsist.

To make matters worse, by May 1945 Germany's industrial centers had been so smashed by protracted Allied strategic bombing that production remained at just 15 percent of prewar levels. The combination of this destruction with the devastated German transport system and the masses of displaced persons meant that in late 1945 the production and distribution of food and goods within Germany proved extremely difficult.

The Allies had strictly to ration whatever meager food supplies remained available to prevent major shortages, and so hunger visited many Germans during the second half of 1945. The delivery of food parcels by the International Red Cross saved the lives of many thousands of destitute Germans, yet despite such efforts, the poor living conditions led to the outbreak of several epidemics that cost the lives of several thousand already malnourished individuals.

Not surprisingly, during summer 1945 it was not just the German economy, but that of the whole of Europe, that bore the terrible scars of the previous five years of war. Total industrial production across the continent during 1946, for example, was just one-third of that in 1938, while European food production remained just one half of its prewar levels. The French economy had declined by one half by 1946, compared to 1938, while that of the Soviet Union had slipped by 13 percent. Indeed, it would take much of Europe until the late 1950s to recover from the disruptions caused by the war.

One of the few 'winners' of the war, however, was the United States, whose economy proved capable of taking advantage of the disrupted international trade flows, and thus grew by some 50 percent during 1941–45. This boom enabled the Americans, from late 1947, to pump $13 billion of Marshall Aid into Europe to rebuild the shattered continent, as part of the Truman Doctrine that offered support to democratic peoples around the world.

The Marshall Aid scheme epitomized the extent to which the international politico-economic influence of Britain and France had declined through their prosecution of the Second World War, and how much that of America had grown. Indeed, during the 1950s it was clear that there were now just two superpowers – the Americans and Soviets. Of course, it would take years for the former European colonial powers fully to recognize their own decline – with Britain, for example, only doing so after the humiliation of the abortive 1956 Suez intervention. Undoubtedly, the costs of the war, the contribution made by the colonies,

The vast destruction and dislocation inflicted on the Reich during the last months of the war left the victorious Allies with an immense burden: how to feed the millions of German refugees and displaced persons. Here, British troops supervise the distribution of food to hungry German refugees. (Imperial War Museum BN 2698)

and the puncturing of the myth of the 'white man's superiority' all fostered powerful anti-colonial insurgencies during 1946–67 that hastened the European powers' 'retreat from empire.'

Meanwhile, for the German people during 1945–49, their fate lay entirely in the hands of the occupying powers, since their state had effectively ceased to exist. Although at Potsdam the four Allied powers had agreed to execute uniformly the principles that underpinned their occupation – demilitarization, deNazification, deindustrialization, decentralization, and democratization – the implementation of these tenets varied enormously between the zones. These differences increased during 1946–48, as the cooperation evident in late 1945 between East and West degenerated into suspicion.

In the three western-controlled sectors of Germany, the locals generally encountered a severe, but largely reasonable administration. However, some interned German military personnel received fairly harsh treatment, for in the emotive last period of the war not even the Western Allies proved immune from the desire for vengeance on the vanquished Nazi regime. The American Treasury Secretary Hans Morgenthau, for example, suggested deindustrializing Germany completely to prevent it ever again being capable of waging aggressive war, while British Prime Minister Winston Churchill suggested summarily executing 100,000 leading Nazis. In reality, such excesses did not occur in the western occupation zone.

In the Soviet-controlled sector, however, the life of ordinary Germans was extremely harsh. Such severity was not surprising, given the terrible privations that the Soviets had suffered during the war, and the heinous occupation policies that the Germans had implemented within Nazi-occupied Soviet territory. Understandably, the Soviets wished to extract recompense for these losses when they occupied eastern Germany, and so implemented a *de facto* reparations policy by either shipping industrial plants back

east, or else systematically exploiting them *in situ* for the benefit of the Soviet state. This policy, which breached several Allied understandings, was one of the principal reasons for the growing division that emerged between the Western Allies and Soviets during 1947. The ruthlessness with which the Soviets exploited their zone in Germany certainly caused many thousands of Germans to succumb to disease brought about by malnutrition and physical hardship.

Another facet of the Allied administration of Germany was deNazification, the process of both 'cleansing' the German people of the 'disease' of Nazism and seeking justice for the terrible crimes committed by the Nazis. The most prominent part of this process was the indicting of German war criminals in the Nuremberg International Tribunal. This court prosecuted 22 senior German political and military leaders on the counts of conspiracy to conduct aggressive war, crimes against peace, war crimes, and crimes against humanity. The third count revolved around the barbarous German war-fighting methods seen especially in the east, while count four related mainly to the genocidal policies of the Holocaust that destroyed the majority of Europe's Jewish population, some 5.5 million human beings. After an 11-month trial, the court sentenced 12 of the defendants to death, and three to life imprisonment, while also condemning the Gestapo and SS as criminal organizations.

In addition to the high-profile Nuremberg proceedings, during 1945–47 the Western Allies carried out thousands of de-Nazification hearings against lesser figures, including members of the criminal organizations condemned at Nuremberg. At these hearings, convicted individuals received sentences of one or two years in a deNazification camp. In contrast, Soviet courts in this period sentenced, in rather arbitrary fashion, several million German prisoners of war to the standard Stalinist 'tenner' – 10 years' forced labor in the infamous camps of the Gulag Archipelago. Only 60 percent of these German prisoners survived their 'tenner' to return to Germany in the mid-1950s.

The Nuremberg process epitomized the desire evident within the 'Big Four' during 1945–46 to establish effective Allied cooperation that would help produce a new, more stable, international environment. The Allies' creation of the United Nations (UN) in June 1945, with an initial membership of 50 states, encapsulated this desire. Replacing the defunct League of Nations, this organization sought to help states peacefully resolve their differences, thus saving mankind from the 'scourge of war.' In addition, the UN would help promote international economic development and the spread of democratization. Such efforts mirrored those undertaken in the wake of the 'total wars' of 1792–1815 and 1914–18 to create international institutions that would help promote peace and prosperity. While the UN has had its failures, in the decades since 1945 the organization has clearly contributed to ensuring a more stable and prosperous international system.

During 1946–47, however, the effective cooperation evident in late 1945 between the Western Allies and their Soviet partners over both the founding of the UN and the administration of Germany degenerated into mistrust. This was epitomized by Churchill's

March 1946 warning that an 'Iron Curtain' was coming down over Soviet-occupied eastern Europe. As the Soviets tightened their grip on eastern Germany to create a Communist satellite state, the Western Allies increased their cooperation until their three zones coalesced into one entity, termed 'Trizonia.' To help this entity and the other democratic states of western Europe recover their economic vibrancy so that they could resist the threat of Communism, from late 1947 the Americans began to pump Marshall Aid funds into western Europe.

The 1948 Berlin Blockade, during which the Soviets tried to block access to West Berlin, permanently severed any prospects, however remote, of continuing cooperation over Germany. The blockade now pushed the rapidly emerging division of German into western and Soviet-controlled zones into a formalized status. During 1949 these areas became *de facto* independent states – the German Federal and Democratic Republics,

At the Nuremberg International Tribunal, 22 senior German political and military leaders – including Karl Dönitz, Hermann Göring, Alfred Jodl, and Wilhelm Keitel – were tried for the crimes that the Nazi Third Reich had committed over the previous 12 years. Both Jodl and Keitel were subsequently executed for their complicity in the terrible crimes committed by the Nazi regime. (AKG Berlin)

respectively – better known as West and East Germany. Each of these states, however, refused to recognize the existence of the other and both aimed for an eventual reunification of Germany – an ambition not achieved until the end of the Cold War in 1989–90.

Subsequently, during the 1950–53 Korean War, western Europe began to rehabilitate West Germany politically and militarily as a bulwark against the military threat offered by the Communist Warsaw Pact. This process culminated in 1955 with the admission of the German Federal Republic into the North Atlantic Treaty Organization (NATO), the anti-Communist European collective security organization formed in April 1949. The Soviets followed suit by rebuilding East Germany to serve the needs of the Warsaw Pact.

The specter of a Third World War in Europe, therefore, forced both the East and West during 1949–55 to reconstruct their respective parts of the devastated pariah postwar German state. This led directly to the West German 'economic miracle' of the 1960s, a process that – after German reunification in 1990 – helped Germany emerge as the dominant economic force within early twenty-first-century Europe. Clearly, the consequences of a 'total war' such as that of 1939–45 are both complex and long lasting.

All in all, the Second World War in Europe was the most devastating and costly war ever fought. Some 55 million human beings perished in a conflagration that sucked in no fewer than 56 states, excluding colonial possessions. During the five-year conflict, Germany incurred 2.8 million military and 2 million civilian deaths, including 550,000 by Western Allied strategic bombing. The Soviets suffered the worst, with 6.3 million military and perhaps 17 million civilian deaths. Europe's other populations suffered a further 1.8 million military and 10.5 million civilian deaths, the latter including 5.5 million Jews. The three Western Allied powers incurred 700,000 military deaths in the European theater. Financially, too, the burden of the war was crippling, with all the belligerents spending some £326 billion at 1946 prices – equivalent to £2,608 billion at 1980 prices – in prosecuting the conflict.

Whatever the enormity of the victory achieved in stopping Hitler's heinous Nazi regime, it is clear that the price of this triumph was so that high that it would take many of the alleged 'victors' of the war decades to recover from the uniquely appalling experience that was the Second World War in Europe.

Bibliography

Unpublished primary sources

Cabinet Office (CAB) and War Office (WO) Papers, The Public Records Office, Kew. Enemy Document Series (EDS) and Field Marshal B. L. Montgomery [BLM] Papers, Department of Documents, Imperial War Museum, London.

Published primary sources

Bradley, O. N., *A Soldier's Story*, New York, 1951.
de Guingand, Maj.-Gen. F., *Operation Victory*, London, 1947.
Eisenhower, D. D., *Crusade in Europe*, New York, 1948.
Montgomery, B. L., *Normandy to the Baltic*, London, 1947.
Patton, G. S., *War as I Knew It*, Boston, 1947.
Speidel, H., *We Defended Normandy*, London, 1951.

Secondary sources

Balkoski, J., *Beyond the Bridgehead*, Harrisburg, PA, 1989.
Blumenson, M., *Breakout and Pursuit*, Washington, DC, 1961.
Blumenson, M., *The Duel for France, 1944*, Boston, 1963.
Carrell, P. (pseud.) [Paul Karl Schmidt], *Invasion They're Coming!*, London, 1962.
D'Este, C., *Decision in Normandy: The Unwritten Story of Montgomery and the Allied Campaign*, London, 1983.
Doubler, M., *Closing with the Enemy: How GIs Fought the War in Europe*, Lawrence, KA, 1994.
Ellis, Maj. L. F., *Victory in the West*, 2 vols, London, 1960, 1968.
English, J. A., *The Canadian Army and the Normandy Campaign: A Study in the Failure of High Command*, London, 1991.
Hamilton, N., *Monty*, 3 vols, London, 1982–86.
Harrison, G., *Cross Channel Attack*, Washington, DC, 1951.
Hart, R. A., *Clash of Arms: How the Allies Won in Normandy*, Boulder, CO, 2001.
Hart, R. A., 'Feeding Mars: the role of logistics in the German defeat in Normandy, 1944,' *War in History*, vol. 3, no. 4 (Fall 1996), pp. 418–35.
Hart, S. A., *Montgomery and 'Colossal Cracks': The 21st Army Group in Northwest Europe, 1944–45*, Westport, CT, 2000.
Hart, S. A., 'Montgomery, morale, casualty conservation and "colossal cracks": 21st Army Group operational technique in north-west Europe 1944–45,' in B. H. Reid (ed.), *Fighting Power*, London, 1995.
Hastings, M., *Overlord: D-Day and the Battle of Normandy*, London, 1984.
Horne, A. and Montgomery, B., *The Lonely Leader: Monty 1944–1945*, London, 1994.
Keegan, J., *Six Armies in Normandy*, New York, 1982.
Kershaw, R. J., *It Never Snows in September: The German View of Market Garden and the Battle of Arnhem, September 1944*, Ramsbury, England, 1990.
Lamb, R., *Montgomery in Europe 1943–45: Success or Failure?*, London, 1983.
Ryan, C., *The Longest Day*, London, 1960.
Schulman, M., *Defeat in the West*, London, 1968.
Stacey, Col. C. P., *The Victory Campaign*, Ottawa, 1960.
Thompson, R. W., *Montgomery the Field Marshal: A Critical Study*, London, 1969.
Weigley, R. F., *Eisenhower's Lieutenants: The Campaigns of France and Germany 1944–5*, 2 vols, London, 1981.
Whitaker, W. D. and Whitaker, S., *The Battle of the River Scheldt*, London, 1985.

Index

References to illustrations are shown in **bold**.

Aachen 44-45, **45**
Africa, North 16, 23
Air Force, Second Tactical 18
air superiority, Allied 20
airborne divisions, Allied 29
Allied advance in 1945: **54**
Allied Control Commission 88
Allied Expeditionary Forces 17, 18
American forces, 27, **60**, **66-67**, 85
Anglo-Canadian 21st Army Group 17, 41, 43, 48, 53, 56
Anglo-Canadian Second Tactical Air Force 18
Antwerp 46, 48, 49, 77
Ardennes 49
Ardennes counteroffensive 7, 48, 61, 64, 65 see also Bulge, Battle
    of the
Arnhem 61
Arnhem bridge 43, 43 see also Operations, Market-Garden
Atlantic, Battle of the 23
Atlantic Wall 20, 27
Austria 11, 87

Bastogne 51, 61, **62**
Berlin, division of 88
Berlin Blockade 91
Blaskowitz, General Johannes von 52, 53, 85
bocage terrain 33, 34, 36
bombing campaign, Allied 73-76, **76**
    carpet bombing 35, 36, 76
    strategic bombing 25-27
Bradley, General Omar 17-18, **18**, 35, 36, 38, 48, 56-57
Breskens pocket 46-47
Britain, Battle of the 13, **14**
British Army see also Anglo-Canadian 21st Army Group
    VIII Corps 32, 33, 36, 37
    XII Corps 52
    XXX Corps 32, 36, 37, 43, 48, 51, 52-53, 56
    Airborne Division, 1st 43-44
    Airborne Division, 6th 29
    Armored Division, 11th 32
    development 21
    Second Army 17, 48, 56, 58-59
Bulge, Battle of the, 16-25 December 1944: 48-49, **50**, 51-53
    see also Ardennes counteroffensive
Burgett, Private Donald 61, 64-65

Caen 31, **32**, 33-34, 76
Calais 46
Canada 68
Canadian Army 21 see also Anglo-Canadian 21st Army Group
    II Corps 56
    2nd Division 24
    First Army 17, 38, 45, 46-47, 58, 67
    volunteer troops ('Zombies') 68
censorship 78
Chamberlain, Neville **11**
Cherbourg 7, 31-32
Churchill, Winston 17, **88**, 90, 91
Cold War in Europe, emergence of, 1945-57: **87**, 91-92
    see also 'Iron Curtain'
'collateral' damage 72-76
Collins, General 'Lightning' Joe 31-32
Colmar pocket 48, 51, 52
commandos, German 49
concentration camps 58, **59**, 77, **78**
Corlett, Major-General Charles 34
Coutances 36
Crerar, General Henry 17, 45, 68
Czechoslovakia 12, 87

D-Day landings, 6 June 1944: 7, 29, **30**, **31**
    see also Normandy campaign; Operations, Overlord
    aftermath 31-35
    preparations 24
        air attacks 27, 75-76
Dempsey, Lieutenant-General Sir Miles 'Bimbo' 17, 47

Devers, General Jacob 18
Dieppe raid 24
Dietrich, SS Colonel-General Joseph Sepp 49, 51
Dönitz, Grand Admiral Karl 83, **84**, 85, 86, **91**
'Dragon's Teeth' anti-tank obstacles **44**
Dresden 73-74

East Germany 90, 91-92
Eisenhower, General Dwight 17, **18**, 41, 48, 51, 55, 56,
    59, 86

Falaise pocket 38, **39**
'fraternization' 70, **71**
French First Army 18, 48, 52, 58
Friedeberg, Grand Admiral Hans von 85, 86
Frost, Lieutenant-Colonel John 43
Funck, Hans von 38

German army see also Wehrmacht, deficiencies
    LXXXIV Corps 35, 36
    LXXXVIII Corps 19
    armies
        First Army 19
        Sixth Army 14
        Seventh Army 19, 49
        Eleventh Army 57-58, 59
        Twelfth Army 57-58
        Fifteenth Army 19, 45-46, **46**
        Nineteenth Army 19, 52
    army groups
        Army Group B 19, 37-38, 49, 52
        Army Group G 19, 52
        Army Group H 52
        Army Group Upper Rhine 52
    Battle Group Chill 40
    OKW (Armed Forces High Command) reserves 20
    Panzer Army, Fifth 49, 51
    Panzer Army, Sixth 49, 52
    Panzer Corps, XLVII 36, 38
    Panzer Division, 2nd 61
    Panzer Division, 21st 29
    Panzer Division, Lehr 36
    Panzer Group West 19
    Parachute Army, First 40-41, 52, 53, 56
    SS Panzer Corps, I 49, 51
    SS Panzer Corps, II 31, 33, 51
    SS Panzer Division Das Reich, 2nd 77
    SS Panzer Division Hitler Youth, 12th 72
    Volksgrenadier (People's Infantry) Divisions 49
    Volkssturm (Home Guard Militia) **74**
    Westheer (German Army in the West) 27, 37, 40, 44, 48, 49, 51,
        52, 55, 56
German dispositions in the west, 6 June 1944: **19**
German Navy (Kriegsmarine) 20, **23**, 28
German occupation zones agreed 87-88
German preparations for Allied invasion 27-28
German war economy 22
Germany, division of **87**, 90, 91-92
Germany, situation after surrender 88-89 90, 91-92
Gerow, Major-General Leonard 31
'Gold' beach 29
Göring, Reichsmarschall Hermann 84, **91**

Harris, Air Marshal Arthur **24-25**
Hausser, SS Colonel-General Paul 36, 52, 55
Himmler, Reichsführer-SS Heinrich 52, 84
Hitler, Adolf 7, 8, 13, 14, 16, 28, 37, 55-56, 58
Hitler Youth movement 72, **74**
Hodges, General Courtney 54
Holland 58, 70
Holocaust 79, 90 see also Jews of Europe
Hungary 52

invasion preparations, Allied 23-24
'Iron Curtain' 8, 91 see also Cold War in Europe, emergence of,
    1945-57
Italy 16, 27

Jodl, Colonel-General Alfred 56, 86, **91**
'Juno' beach 29

Keitel, Field Marshal Wilhelm 85, **86**, 86, **91**
Kesselring, Field Marshal Albert 55, 58
King, W.L. Mackenzie **17**, 68
Kluge, Field Marshal von 37
Kranke, Admiral 20

La Gleize 51
La Haye-du-Puits 34
Le Havre 46
Leigh-Mallory, Air Chief Marshal Sir Trafford **18**, 18
Leopold Canal 47
losses 47, 48, 51, 53, 55, 92
Luftwaffe 20, 26-27, 28
Lüneburg Heath 85

Malmédy massacre 51
Manteuffel, General Hasso von 49
Maquis (French Resistance) 70, 77
Marshall Aid scheme 89, 91
McBryde, Brenda 80-82
Meijel 47-48
Metz 44, 48
Middleton, Major-General Troy 34
Model, Field Marshal Walther 43, 52, **57**, 57, 58
Molotov-Ribbentrop Pact 13
Montgomery, General Bernard 17, **18**, 21, 31, 32-33, 34, 36, 38, 41, 42, 44, 51, 53, 56, 58, 68, 85
Morgenthau, Hans 90
Mortain **37**, **38**
Munich Agreement (1938) 12

NATO (North Atlantic Treaty Organization) 92
'National Redoubt' 58, 59-60
Normandy 20
    German counteroffensive 37-38
Normandy campaign, 6 June-20 August 1944: **35**
    see also D-Day landings; Operations, Overlord
North Africa 16, 23
North Atlantic Treaty Organization (NATO) 92
Noville 61, 64, 65
Nuremberg War Crimes Tribunal **84**, 86, 90, **91**

Odon, River 32, 33
offensives *see also* Operations
    Grenade 52
    Totalize 38
    Tractable 38
'Omaha' beach 29, 31
Oosterbeek 43, 44
Operations *see also* offensives
    Barbarossa 7, 13
    Blackcock 48, 52
    Bluecoat 36
    Charnwood 33
    Cobra 34, 35-36
    Epsom 32-33
    Goodwood **24-25**, **31**, 34-35
    Infatuate 47
    Kitten 38, 40
    Market-Garden, 17-26 September 1944: **42**, 42-45
    see also Arnhem bridge
    Northwind 51
    Overlord 27, 78 *see also* D-Day landings; Normandy campaign
    Plunder 55, 56-60
    Sea Lion 13
    Switchback 46-47
    Torch 16, 27
    Varsity 56
    Veritable 44, 52
Oppenheim 55
Oradour-sur-Glane massacre 77
Orne River 22, 34

Paris, liberation of **40**
Patton, General George 37, 48, 58, 59
Peiper, SS Lieutenant-Colonel Joachim 49, 51
Pèriers Ridge 29
'Phoney War' 13
Poland 12, 13, 52
Potsdam International Conference 87, **88**, 88, 90
prisoners-of-war, German **45**, 90-91

race issue 66-67
Ramsay, Admiral Sir Bertram **18**, 18
rationing 68-70, **69**
Rauray Bridge 32
Red Army 14, 16

refugees 88
Reichswald Forest 52, 53
Remagen, Ludendorff bridge 53-55
Resistance, French (Maquis) 70, 77
Rhine, River 42, 48, 53-69
Rhineland 11
Roer, River 48, 52, 53
Rommel, Field Marshal Erwin 19, **20**
Roosevelt, President Theodore **17**, 68
Royal Air Force (RAF) 24-26 *see also* Anglo-Canadian Second
    Tactical Air Force
    Bomber Command 18, 25-26, 27, 73-76
Ruhr industrial zone 56-57, 58
Rundstedt, Field Marshal Gerd von **18**, 18-19, 51, 55

St Lô 31, 34, 36
Scheldt estuary 45-46, **46**, 47
Schlemm, Lieutenant-General Alfred 52, 53
Schwammenauel Dam 48, 53
Schweppenburg, General Leo von 19
Seine, River **26**, 38, 40
Siegfried Line **44**, 44, 45, 48, 52, 53
Simonds, Lieutenant-General Guy 45, 47
Skorzeny, SS-Colonel Otto 49
Souleuvre, River 36-37
South Beveland peninsula 46, 47
Soviet advance 59, 85
Soviet forces meet up with American forces **60**, **66-67**, 85
Soviet Union 8, 12-14, 16
    creates Communist satellite regimes 88 *see also* East Germany
Sperrle, General 20
Stalin, Josef 13, 14
Stalingrad **14**, 14
Stoumont 49
Strasbourg 48, 58
strategic situation in Europe, 6 June 1944: **15**
strategy, 21-22, 41
Student, General Kurt 40-41, 56
surrender in Italy 84-85
surrender of German forces 85-86
'Sword' beach 29

Torgau 7, 59, **60**
Trier 53
Triple Alliance (1907) 12
Truman, President **88**

U-boats 23
'Ultra' codes 20, 38
United Nations 91
United States Army 22, 27
    29th Division 34
    Airborne Division, 82nd 29
    Airborne Division, 101st 29, 51, 61, 64
        506th Parachute Infantry Regiment 61, 64
    armies
        First Army 17, 34, 35, 37, 44, 48, 51, 53-54, 57, 59
        Third Army 17-18, 44, 48, 53, 58, 59
        Seventh Army 18, 48, 55, 58, 59-60
        Ninth Army 18, 48, 51, 52, 57, 59
        Fifteenth Army 18
    Armored Division, 11th 37
    Army Group, 6th 18, 48
    Army Group, 12th 17, 37, 44
    corps
        V Corps 31, 38, 48
        VII Corps 31, 34, 36, 48
        VIII Corps 34, 36
        XII Corps 55
        XIX Corps 34, 36
        XX Corps 55
United States Army Air Force 26, 73-76
    IX Tactical Air Command 18
    XIX Tactical Air Command 18
    Eighth Air Force 18
'Utah' beach 29, 31

V1 'Vengeance' rocket attacks 76-77
V2 ballistic missiles 41, 42, 77
VE-Day (Victory in Europe Day) **66-67**

Walcheren island **47**, 47
Wesel 53, 56
Weser, River 56
West Germany 91-92
West Wall 7, **44**, 44
Wolff, SS Colonel-General Karl 84
women's contribution to war effort 70, **72-73**, 72

Zeeland 45-46

Related titles from Osprey Publishing

CAMPAIGN (CAM)
**Strategies, tactics and battle experiences
of opposing armies**

0850459214	CAM 001	NORMANDY 1944
0850459583	CAM 003	FRANCE 1940
0850459591	CAM 005	ARDENNES 1944
1855322110	CAM 016	KURSK 1943
1855322536	CAM 018	GUADALCANAL 1942
1855323028	CAM 024	ARNHEM 1944
1855324784	CAM 042	BAGRATION 1944
184176390X	CAM 062	PEARL HARBOR 1941 (WITH CD)
1855329670	CAM 073	OPERATION COMPASS 1940
1855329999	CAM 074	THE RHINELAND 1945
1841760897	CAM 075	LORRAINE 1944
1841761028	CAM 077	TARAWA 1943
1841760927	CAM 080	TOBRUK 1941
1841761788	CAM 081	IWO JIMA 1945
1841762962	CAM 088	OPERATION COBRA 1944
1841762318	CAM 092	ST NAZAIRE 1942
1855326078	CAM 096	OKINAWA 1945

WARRIOR (WAR)
**Motivation, training, combat experiences
and equipment of individual soldiers**

1855322889	WAR 002	WAFFEN-SS SOLDIER 1940–45
1855328429	WAR 026	US PARATROOPER 1941–45
1841763128	WAR 036	GREY WOLF: U-BOAT CREWMAN OF WORLD WAR II
1841763276	WAR 037	GERMAN SEAMAN 1939–45
1841763268	WAR 038	FALLSCHIRMJÄGER: GERMAN PARATROOPER 1935–45
1841763306	WAR 045	US INFANTRYMAN IN WORLD WAR II (1)
		PACIFIC AREA OF OPERATIONS 1941–45
1841763284	WAR 046	PANZER CREWMAN 1939–45

ELITE (ELI)
**Uniforms, equipment, tactics and personalities
of troops and commanders**

0850459486	ELI 031	US ARMY AIRBORNE 1940–90
1855322951	ELI 046	US ARMY AIR FORCE (1)
1855323397	ELI 051	US ARMY AIR FORCE (2)
1855324970	ELI 059	US MARINE CORPS 1941–45
1855325462	ELI 061	THE GUARDS DIVISIONS 1914–45
1855325799	ELI 064	ARMY COMMANDOS 1940–45
1841761419	ELI 068	THE MILITARY SNIPER SINCE 1914
1841761958	ELI 079	THE ROYAL NAVY 1939–45
1841763012	ELI 080	THE US NAVY IN WORLD WAR II

MEN-AT-ARMS (MAA)
**Uniforms, equipment, history
and organisation of troops**

0850454344	MAA 024	THE PANZER DIVISIONS
0850454255	MAA 034	THE WAFFEN-SS
0850453593	MAA 103	GERMANY'S SPANISH VOLUNTEERS 1941–45
0850454174	MAA 117	THE POLISH ARMY 1939–45
0850454336	MAA 124	GERMAN COMMANDERS OF WORLD WAR II
0850454751	MAA 131	GERMANY'S EASTERN FRONT ALLIES 1941–45
0850454808	MAA 139	GERMAN AIRBORNE TROOPS 1939–45
0850455243	MAA 147	FOREIGN VOLUNTEERS OF THE WEHRMACHT 1941–45
0850457394	MAA 187	BRITISH BATTLE INSIGNIA (2) 1939–45
0850459028	MAA 213	GERMAN MILITARY POLICE UNITS 1939–45
0850459397	MAA 216	THE RED ARMY OF THE GREAT PATRIOTIC WAR 1941–45
0850459443	MAA 220	THE SA 1921–45: HITLER'S STORMTROOPERS
0850459664	MAA 225	THE ROYAL AIR FORCE 1939–45
0850459524	MAA 234	GERMAN COMBAT EQUIPMENTS 1939–45
185532136X	MAA 238	FOREIGN VOLUNTEERS OF THE ALLIED FORCES 1939–45
1855321696	MAA 246	THE ROMANIAN ARMY OF WORLD WAR II
1855323583	MAA 266	THE ALLGEMEINE-SS
1855324466	MAA 270	FLAGS OF THE THIRD REICH (1) WEHRMACHT
1855324598	MAA 278	FLAGS OF THE THIRD REICH (3) PARTY AND POLICE UNITS
1855326396	MAA 311	THE GERMAN ARMY 1939–45 (1) BLITZKRIEG
1855326663	MAA 315	THE FRENCH ARMY 1939–45 (1)
185532640X	MAA 316	THE GERMAN ARMY 1939–45 (2) N. AFRICA & BALKANS
1855327074	MAA 318	THE FRENCH ARMY 1939–45 (2)
1855327619	MAA 325	FRENCH FOREIGN LEGION 1914–1945
1855327953	MAA 326	THE GERMAN ARMY 1939–45 (3) EASTERN FRONT 1941–43
1855327961	MAA 330	THE GERMAN ARMY 1939–45 (4) EASTERN FRONT 1943–45
185532797X	MAA 336	THE GERMAN ARMY 1939–45 (5) WESTERN FRONT
185532864X	MAA 340	THE ITALIAN ARMY 1940–45 (1) EUROPE 1940–43
1855329956	MAA 342	THE US ARMY IN WORLD WAR II (1) THE PACIFIC
1841760854	MAA 347	THE US ARMY IN WORLD WAR II (2) THE MEDITERRANEAN
1855328658	MAA 349	THE ITALIAN ARMY 1940–45 (2) AFRICA 1940–43
1841760862	MAA 350	THE US ARMY IN WORLD WAR II (3) NORTH-WEST EUROPE
1855328666	MAA 353	THE ITALIAN ARMY 1940–45 (3) ITALY 1943–45
1841760528	MAA 354	THE BRITISH ARMY 1939–45 (1) NORTH WEST EUROPE
1841760536	MAA 357	WORLD WAR II ALLIED WOMEN'S SERVICES
1841763020	MAA 359	CANADIAN FORCES IN WORLD WAR II
1841763233	MAA 361	AXIS CAVALRY IN WORLD WAR II
1841763535	MAA 362	THE JAPANESE ARMY 1931–45 (1) 1931–42
1841761931	MAA 363	GERMANY'S EASTERN FRONT ALLIES (2) BALTIC FORCES
1841763527	MAA 365	WORLD WAR II GERMAN BATTLE INSIGNIA

ORDER OF BATTLE (OOB)
**Unit-by-unit troop movements and
command strategies of major battles**

1855328534	OOB 004	THE ARDENNES OFFENSIVE VI PANZER ARMEE: NORTHERN SECTOR
1855328542	OOB 005	THE ARDENNES OFFENSIVE V US CORPS & XVIII US (AIRBORNE) CORPS: NORTHERN SECTOR
1855328577	OOB 008	THE ARDENNES OFFENSIVE V PANZER ARMEE: CENTRAL SECTOR
1855328585	OOB 009	THE ARDENNES OFFENSIVE US VII & VIII CORPS AND BRITISH XXX CORPS: CENTRAL SECTOR
1855329131	OOB 012	THE ARDENNES OFFENSIVE I ARMEE & VII ARMEE: SOUTHERN SECTOR
185532914X	OOB 013	THE ARDENNES OFFENSIVE US III & XII CORPS: SOUTHERN SECTOR

ESSENTIAL HISTORIES (ESS)
**Concise overviews of major wars
and theatres of war**

1841762296	ESS 018	THE SECOND WORLD WAR (1) THE PACIFIC

NEW VANGUARD (NVG)
**Design, development and operation
of the machinery of war**

185532296X	NVG 003	SHERMAN MEDIUM TANK 1942–45
1855322978	NVG 004	CHURCHILL INFANTRY TANK 1941–51
1855323370	NVG 005	TIGER I HEAVY TANK 1942–45
1855323966	NVG 007	IS-2 HEAVY TANK 1944–73
1855324571	NVG 008	MATILDA INFANTRY TANK 1938–45
1855323826	NVG 009	T-34/76 MEDIUM TANK 1941–45
1855324679	NVG 011	M3 INFANTRY HALF-TRACK 1940–73
1855325128	NVG 014	CRUSADER CRUISER TANK 1939–45
1855324962	NVG 017	KV-1 & 2 HEAVY TANKS 1939–45
1855325357	NVG 020	T-34-85 MEDIUM TANK 1944–94
1855324768	NVG 022	PANTHER VARIANTS 1942–45
1855328461	NVG 025	SDKFZ 251 HALF-TRACK 1939–45
1855328445	NVG 026	GERMAN LIGHT PANZERS 1932–42
1855328453	NVG 027	PANZERKAMPFWAGEN III MEDIUM TANK 1936–44
1855328437	NVG 028	PANZERKAMPFWAGEN IV MEDIUM TANK 1936–45
1855328496	NVG 029	GERMAN ARMOURED CARS AND RECONNAISSANCE HALF-TRACKS 1939–45
185532850X	NVG 030	AMTRACS US AMPHIBIOUS ASSAULT VEHICLES
1855329115	NVG 033	M3 & M5 STUART LIGHT TANK 1940–45
1841760048	NVG 034	STURMARTILLERIE & PANZERJÄGER 1939–45
1841761354	NVG 036	JAGDPANZER 38 'HETZER' 1944–45
1841761826	NVG 037	STURMGESCHÜTZ III AND IV 1942–45
184176341 1	NVG 046	88 MM FLAK 18/36/37/41 AND PAK 43 1936–45
1841763500	NVG 048	THE 25-POUNDER FIELD GUN 1939–72

AIRCRAFT OF THE ACES (ACES)
Experiences and achievements of 'ace' fighter pilots

AVIATION ELITE (AEU)
Combat histories of fighter or bomber units

COMBAT AIRCRAFT (COM)
History, technology and crews of military aircraft
Contact us for details of titles in these series – see below

To order any of these titles, or for more information on Osprey Publishing, contact:

Osprey Direct (UK)   *Tel:* +44 (0)1933 443863   *Fax:* +44 (0)1933 443849   *E-mail:* info@ospreydirect.co.uk

Osprey Direct (USA) c/o MBI Publishing   *Toll-free:* 1 800 826 6600   *Phone:* 1 715 294 3345

Fax: 1 715 294 4448   *E-mail:* info@ospreydirectusa.com

www.ospreypublishing.com

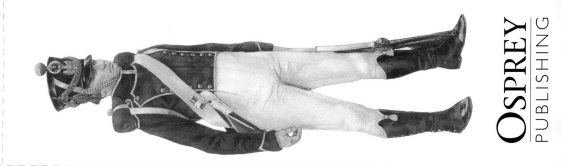

FIND OUT MORE ABOUT OSPREY

❏ Please send me a FREE trial issue of Osprey Military Journal

❏ Please send me the latest listing of Osprey's publications

❏ I would like to subscribe to Osprey's e-mail newsletter

Title/rank _____

Name _____

Address _____

_____

_____

_____

Postcode/zip _____

State/country _____

E-mail _____

Which book did this card come from?

_____

❏ I am interested in military history

My preferred period of military history is _____

❏ I am interested in military aviation

My preferred period of military aviation is _____

I am interested in (please tick all that apply)

❏ general history   ❏ militaria   ❏ model making

❏ wargaming   ❏ re-enactment

Please send to:

USA & Canada:
Osprey Direct USA, c/o MBI Publishing,
PO Box 1, 729 Prospect Ave, Osceola, WI 54020, USA

UK, Europe and rest of world:
Osprey Direct UK, PO Box 140, Wellingborough,
Northants, NN8 2FA, United Kingdom

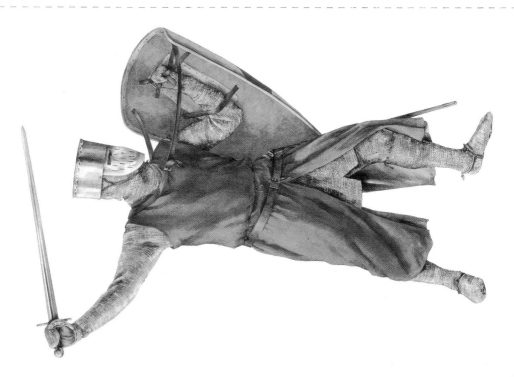

OSPREY
PUBLISHING

www.ospreypublishing.com

call our telephone hotline
for a free information pack

USA & Canada: 1-800-826-6600
UK, Europe and rest of world call:
+44 (0) 1933 443 863

Young Guardsman
Figure taken from *Warrior 22:
Imperial Guardsman 1799–1815*
Published by Osprey
Illustrated by Christa Hook

POSTCARD

Knight, c.1190
Figure taken from *Warrior 1: Norman Knight 950 – 1204AD*
Published by Osprey
Illustrated by Christa Hook